SHARIKA ESTHER SHARMA is h
in Washington D.C., USA, ;
part of her life. After gradua
School in Mussoorie, Sharika went on to acquire her Bachelor's
degree in Mass Communication and English Literature from
the University of San Diego, California. Returning to India, she
wrote articles on latest archaeological discoveries for *The Asian
Age* and *Education Times*. She has written for television and was
part of a production for Star Plus channel. She took a sabbatical
after giving birth to her two sons.

More recently, she has written an article for the blog
fempowermentawards.com called 'Kali's Significance in the 21st
Century'. She travels between her homes in Delhi and Mumbai
for work. Her novel, *Unchain My Heart*, will be released in 2022.

Monkeys in My Garden: Reflections from a Life in Isolation is
her first book.

Praise For The Book

"The intertwining of a multifaceted memoir with the pandemic makes *Monkeys in My Garden* such an interesting read. Reality as we know it during the pandemic criss-crosses with the narrative of Sharika Sharma's life, leaving an indelible mark of a complex reality that enthrals from beginning to end."

—Nina Rajan Pillai, entrepreneur

"Having known Sharika Sharma and her fine family for ages, I always saw a streak of anecdotal brilliance in her. Her ability to whip up wit and lace it with relevance has been her birthmark for as long as I know. To then wrap it in an envelope, of some fine humorous writing, is a feat that only Sharika could have achieved. While the lockdown may have affected many in ways which are negative and depressing, Sharika has unlocked her potential as a brilliant story-teller in *Monkeys in My Garden*. A book dedicated to the indomitable human spirit and the ability of all of us to have a laugh as we relive memories long gone by."

—Suhel Seth, author, advertising professional and entrepreneur

"A talented writer. A well-written book. Sharika is a fine raconteur."

—Kamal Nath, senior Congress leader, former chief minister of Madhya Pradesh

Monkeys in My Garden

Reflections from a Life in Isolation

Sharika Esther Sharma

Om Books International

First published in 2022 by

Om Books International

Corporate & Editorial Office
A-12, Sector 64, Noida 201 301
Uttar Pradesh, India
Phone: +91 120 477 4100
Email: editorial@ombooks.com
Website: www.ombooksinternational.com

Sales Office
107, Ansari Road, Darya Ganj,
New Delhi 110 002, India
Phone: +91 11 4000 9000
Fax: +91 11 2327 8091
Email: sales@ombooks.com
Website: www.ombooks.com

ISBN: 978-93-92834-01-1

Printed in India

10 9 8 7 6 5 4 3 2 1

I dedicate this book to the frontline workers and good Samaritans that risked their lives and that lost their lives in trying to save the lives of their fellow men, women and children during the Covid pandemic.

"The smallest act of kindness is worth more than the greatest intention"-Kahlil Gibran

Day 1

21 March 2020

The day the mayor of New York declared a state of emergency, I knew India was headed for trouble. I fretted for my husband and children, and the city we lived in, bustling with 22 million people. I was sure the disease that had brought New York to its knees would spread like a blaze in a wicker house when it reached Mumbai.

My first book had taken me several years to write, thanks to my other—and bigger—job as a mother of two headstrong boys. I was looking forward eagerly to embarking on my next literary adventure. But the adventure in store for me, for all of humanity, was to be of an altogether different nature. A deadly disease that allegedly started in a wildlife market in Wuhan in the Republic of China, had spread to South Korea, Italy, France, Spain, Iran, UK and America. In a matter of time, it would make landfall in India, giving precious little time to prepare.

I decided to leave the city with my sons. Their spring break had begun and, I gathered, if a lockdown was to be announced—as it had been in other countries—it would be better for the boys to be at their grandparents' farmhouse outside Delhi than in a two-bedroom flat in Mumbai. Choosing to stay behind with his parents, my husband booked our tickets. Two days later, we were bidding him farewell. Looking into his chocolate-coloured eyes, I hoped to be reunited with him soon, though I had an uncanny feeling it would be a while... a *long* while... I hoped I had made the right decision.

By the time I settled my sons into their room at the house, Donald Trump had declared the virus outbreak a national emergency, and the World Health Organisation (WHO) warned that Europe had become its epicentre.

There are three houses at the farm, one housing my parents, another my brother and his family, and when I visit, my family; and the third is where my aunt, whom I affectionately call *bua*, lives. Each house is surrounded by a lawn and there is a swimming pool beside the one that my brother and I stay in, called A-Block. There are five staff quarters at the back of the property, and beside a border wall is my mother's art studio.

I was determined to exercise a lockdown at the farm, even before the Prime Minister appeared on television and advised "social distancing", a phrase none of us had heard before. Most vehemently opposed to the idea of staying home was my father, a 73-year-old cancer survivor. He was in the habit of going for an ice cream every day to his friend's hotel, and then visiting the Congress office, where he got to meet workers from his former constituency. As a retired politician no longer in the fray, he missed the action.

My father set out on his daily excursion as my mother went to her studio and closed herself in with her art.

Day 2

22 March 2020

The curfew today coincides with calls on Japan from the international community to cancel the Olympic Games, scheduled to take place in Tokyo this summer.

I'm alarmed to see that, in spite of the curfew, people are milling around in marketplaces and politicians are continuing to hold public meetings. A wedding in Telangana hosted a thousand guests. Two temples in South India held their annual festivals. Replete with decked-up elephants and musicians in costumes pounding on their instruments, the processions were flanked by food stalls crammed with devotees. They all appeared to be blissfully oblivious of the public announcements that celebrities are making on social media, urging people to stay at home.

I awoke this morning to the conspicuous absence of noise. The void that the usual sounds of vehicles, honking and human voices left behind was filled with birdsong and time ticking rhythmically at my bedside. The dogs seemed to know that something was off; they weren't barking. If only I wasn't aware of the awful thing that was happening, I could have enjoyed the precious silence. Knowing made me want to hibernate under my blanket until it all passed. I wanted God to save us, like he had saved the Israelites when he "passed over" their houses during the 10th plague of the Egyptians. But asking God for salvation made me feel like a hypocrite.

The Wuhan market, where the pandemic allegedly originated, was a wet market, where wild animals from all over the world were kept in cages, stacked one on top of the other, to be slaughtered and sold as food. The animals in the cages at the bottom were perpetually drenched in the excrement, pus and blood dripping from the animals in the cages above, until they too were slaughtered. The worst viruses humanity has known, had jumped from animals to humans. This pandemic was inevitable; it was waiting to happen.

In the 1970s, China was hit by a famine that killed 36 million people and left another 100 million starving. To alleviate hunger, the government allowed private farming of wild animals. Smaller farmers started catching and raising animals like turtles and snakes to feed the populace. In 1988, the country enacted the Wildlife Protection Law, designating wild animals as resources protected by the state. This meant that they could be used for both trade and human consumption. The passing of the law led to industrial-sized operations in raising a variety of animals, like deer, bears, foxes, badgers, lizards and bats. The wet market in Wuhan had 75 species under one roof. There were hundreds like it all over the country. The trade provided cover for illegal wildlife trafficking in tigers, rhinoceros and pangolins, to name a few endangered animals.

In view of our collective human attitude and behaviour regarding animals, the question arises, "Do we deserve salvation?" When I read about the doctors and nurses fighting on the frontline, risking their lives to save the lives of strangers, I'm tempted to reply, "Yes". But when I think of how we've treated animals on the planet, and indeed, the planet itself, mining, fencing it in, trashing it, I'm not so sure. Who gave us the right to snatch forest land from wild animals, poach them, cull them or eat them? Certainly not God! Is it any wonder that the disease snuffing us out like flies originated in an animal market? It is said to have jumped from an infected wild animal to a human who ate its meat. AIDS, too, jumped to a hunter who killed and ate an infected chimpanzee. Really, do we need to eat chimpanzees?

The industrial farms in Wuhan kept hundreds of highly evolved mammals in cages so small they couldn't turn around or stretch their legs. The bear, for instance, is a sensitive, intelligent mammal. Bears are affectionate towards their young and tend to them with great care. Is this the treatment they deserve? We let it happen. We let it all happen. We filled the oceans with naval and cargo ships until their clamour drove whales to beach themselves and die, rather than go insane with the mixed messages they were receiving from ships and not their kin. We polluted the waters and turned whole stretches of the oceans into dead zones.

Did we cry for the bears or the whales? Did their pain make us alter our ways? So why are we crying for ourselves and calling out to God to save us? What gave us the right to wear wild animals as fur, use their glands to make perfume, or lock them up? What will it take to teach us that wild animals belong in the wild and not in cruel cages—a virus, a pandemic, the erasure of the human race from the face of the earth?

We went about our lives, hoarding, vacationing, partying, raising animals in the most inhumane conditions, and throwing tons of food we couldn't eat or didn't want, into the trash. We knew about the mass murders happening in Yemen and Syria but saw it as someone else's problem. The deforestation in the

Amazon, the lungs of our planet, the fires that killed a million wild animals in Australia and thousands more in California—we watched aghast, and a few weeks later, were back to business as usual. Who am I to say? An expert, an activist, a celebrity? I am the guilty party. And *this* is my litany of repentance.

We poked fun at people like Greta Thunberg for upping the ante on the climate crisis, and at Prince Charles for talking to trees. What made us think the trees couldn't hear the prince? We chose not to listen to the voices of reason when they cried themselves hoarse, warning us about what we were doing. Our desires, our ridiculous woes, our pleasures; that was all we were focused on. Now, when it is our turn to be locked up, forced to face our follies, will we change our ways?

Day 3

23 March 2020

When my brother Suveer got married, the house that's referred to as A-Block—the one with the pool—was extended. Three bedrooms, two bathrooms and a kitchen were constructed for his family. My sons, Robin and Rishi, and his son, Tin Tin, and daughter, Shona, are all below the age of 12; Robin being the eldest and Shona the youngest.

The grown-ups sit and chat while the children pound away on their remote controls in front of the Play Station in Tin Tin's room. We talk about our family in Delhi, Mumbai and beyond, while trying to stay upbeat by sharing jokes on social media and watching humorous videos made by people in lockdown. I got a phone call from a friend from Mumbai to tell me that she's moved to Delhi with her husband and two small children. Her parents live in the Netherlands and their farmhouse was empty; a safe place to be. It's right across the street from us. I offer to send her books and my kids' old toys. Nehru vest over a crisp white kurta-pyjama, my father enters the room, ready to go for his rounds. He went out yesterday, too, during curfew.

This time, I try a different approach to dissuade him from leaving. "Dad," I say, "if your driver is stopped, you can expect a line in the newspaper tomorrow that reads something like: *Prominent Veteran Politician Found Traipsing Around the City, Defying the Curfew and Breaking the Law."* All of us had a laugh. All but dad. The attempt to stop him was fruitless. Off he went.

Allegedly, 40% of politicians suffer from obsessive compulsive disorder. I guess one has to be singular in their thinking to get a tough job done. It helps to be committed, perseverant and patient when you are a politician, and obsessive. To get my father to change his routine will be no easy task: we may have to shackle him to a post to stop him from leaving the farm. For him, every day is Christmas Day. How blissful it must be to live with your head in the sand, oblivious of reality, even when it's hammering you in the haunches! He's always been his own man, going where he wants and doing as he wills. I so wished, as a child, to get quality time with my father and both my brother and I longed to have meaningful conversations with him. He was inaccessible. Whatever he knew about us he knew only from what he was told, which was usually unfavourable.

When we were teenagers, my parents had four Great Danes at the farm. They ran around like stray dogs, unruly, untrained and ferocious. One of them pounced on a servant once and tore his mouth; the young man needed plastic surgery to patch it up. When his stitches healed, he had a permanent smile on his face, like the Joker from *The Dark Knight*. We siblings too had negligible discipline. As a 15-year-old, I had a Gypsy jeep that I'd drive to my friends' houses whenever I pleased. I drank with buds much older than myself and participated in races on the open roads in the dead of night. I lived in the Gypsy and I lived like a gypsy. Nobody knew where I was going or when I came home. Suffice to say, I survived my adolescence. I have the fine education my parents provided me at a prestigious boarding school—and the dedicated teachers therein—to thank for my salvation.

The family came together to cut the vanilla cake I had baked for Robin today, his 12th birthday. My mother had emerged from her art studio after three days, purple and red paint under her chipped nails. If you were to step into the prodigious brick structure that looked like a train tunnel from the inside and a pipe half buried in the ground from the outside—which was her studio—you would find surreal, realistic and abstract paintings of varying sizes, resting on easels lined in a row. You'd come upon a plump rooster perched on a leafy branch—bright, vivacious, eyeing you curiously; a langur casually peeling a banana, snakes, frogs, portraits of pet poodles, cats and rhesus macaques. You'd also find life-size sculptures of dogs with flowers painted on them and of children and horses.

My mother has a talent for painting animals and giving them personality. Tearing herself away from her private haven, she was the last to join the group assembled around the table in the garden. We ate my son's birthday cake under the watchful gaze of a huddle of monkeys up in a tree, and the singing of birds, which was now a constant.

Twelve states and union territories have gone into lockdown. I'm converting the wooden playroom under a tree in the lawn into a sick room. If I fall ill, I can stay there. I need to get a mattress and a pillow, and separate utensils for it. I need AAA batteries and light bulbs, notebooks and pens. I've also got a whole list of foodstuffs and medical supplies that need to be bought. To avoid detection by the police, my driver Bhikam Singh who lives in Gurgaon (Gurugram) in the neighbouring state of Haryana, took the narrow streets of villages on his motorcycle to get to the farm. I consider him one of the heroes fighting on the frontline—drivers, garbage collectors, airline workers, policemen and medical personnel who are risking their lives to help everyone else save theirs.

Bhikam Singh got into my car and cruised along the wide and empty streets of Delhi, wearing a mask and a pair of surgical gloves, going from one general store to the next to buy me the things I needed.

It's springtime and the flowers are blooming. I watch a hummingbird flit from a bush to a tree past my window. Though I feel lucky to be locked in a place like this, I can't help but think about my husband back in Mumbai. The city is a ticking time bomb. I worry about my friends and neighbours, my children's teachers, classmates and their parents. Close to 45% of the population of Mumbai lives in slums. The residents of these slums work in and deliver goods to the housing societies. Vegetable vendors, sanitation workers, delivery men, drivers, dhobis; they all live in these cities within the city, made up of tiny rooms accommodating five or six people—sometimes more—separated by gullies, yielding barely enough space to walk in single file.

I worry for my driver in Mumbai, Santosh, who's worked for me for eight years. He lives with his wife and three children in one such tiny room. In about two months, the clouds will swell and a flood of water will fill the city from the sky and sea. The slums will float as if on a raft. Diseases will spread, as they always do. And if this disease, the mother of all diseases, isn't contained by then, the situation will be potentially cataclysmic. Now, at this precise point, I could be called a pessimist. I *will* be called a pessimist—like Giordano Bruno was, for claiming the universe was infinite and that other solar systems existed. He was burnt at the stake for it. We humans, by nature, fear the unknown. "Infinite" is a big word. Poor Bruno.

If I'm considered a pessimist for planning for a future that is uncertain, I can live with it. I'm in good company. In 2015, Bill Gates gave a TED Talk, warning world leaders about the likelihood of a virus threatening the existence of the human race. We've invested so much money in nuclear deterrence, he said, but what we should be investing in is a "system to stop an epidemic". We should be investing in germ games and not war games, he said, warning that "the failure to prepare could allow the next epidemic to be dramatically more devastating than Ebola". He might as well have been talking to trees.

India, a country with over a billion people, continued, even after this talk, to spend only 3% of its GDP on healthcare. Why should Prince Charles take all the flak for talking to trees! None of the world leaders followed Gates's advice, though his IQ is higher than most people, and, in some cases, a number of world leaders combined. He advised them to consult epidemiologists and put a response system in place. He told them that we had the science and the technology to do it. But, unfortunately for all of us, their motto is to act only *after* a disaster strikes; ban wildlife food markets only *after* a major pandemic kills thousands of people and devastates the world economy. We didn't learn from AIDS. We didn't learn from Ebola. The SARS virus wasn't bad enough. It took this monster virus, the killer of 2020, to do it. All those epidemics resulted when humans consumed bushmeat. 75% of all epidemics recorded in history, in fact, originated in wild animals.

Leadership—that's what it comes down to. We, the people; we are responsible for what happens to us. To elect good leaders, we have to be aware of what's happening in our world and what our leaders are going to do about it. Awareness and leadership are going to be critical to our existence as a human race when it all starts over again, because it will literally have to start over again when this disease is done with its business of destruction.

Day 4

24 March 2020

We moved into the farm when I was 12, the same year I joined boarding school. The farm was my home until I got married at the age of 30. As long as the old cook from before my marriage was there, all was well; it continued to feel like home. But when he left, or rather, was driven away after my grandmother died, my sister-in-law hired a new cook. Fissures tend to arise in families under unnatural circumstances; and rarely does a circumstance get more unnatural than a nationwide lockdown. Today, the first crack occurred in A-Block's kitchen. The cook complained to my sister-in-law about my children. He was unhappy about having to heat milk for them at night, and other similar tasks I'm not aware of.

I brought someone from Mumbai to help me with my boys, an 18-year-old named Sonu, but the new cook was not satisfied, even though Sonu chopped the vegetables and washed the dishes. The cook was used to getting four hours of rest during the day, but now that he was getting only three hours, he was hot and bothered. Weighing 95 kilos, he finds cooking for an extra four persons an added load, forgetting that he was washing the dishes and chopping the vegetables before we arrived. It all sounds so petty—it hurts my fingers to write about it—but because of this lazy man, I got an earful from my brother.

In these extraordinary circumstances, my chief priority is the safety of my children. I am convinced that this lockdown will continue, periodically, into the next year. And that means I will have to stay at the farm until it is safe enough to travel. I *have* to make it work. I don't have the luxury to marvel at how the place I once took for granted as home was no longer home to me. It is our culture that does this to us women after marriage. We become second-class citizens, not only in our parental homes but, if we have our in-laws living in the same house—like I do—more often than not, in our marital homes too. Home becomes a battleground. And in a scenario like this, when everyone is locked up together, the cracks under the plaster of Paris exterior, under the niceness and social decorum, start to get exposed. Pretensions shed and the pent-up shit oozes through the cracks and starts to stink up the place.

My sons spoke to their classmates on the phone this morning. Most of them are cooped up in their two or three-bedroom flats. They're not allowed to step outside to meet their friends or kick a ball or even walk their dogs. I spent so much time in Mumbai caring for my children and the house that I had precious little left to do what I wanted, which was to read and write. I declined invitations from school moms to luncheons or Diwali dinners to save time for myself. After speaking to them and taking their guidance on homeschooling over the past week, I swore to myself that, when this thing was over, I would accept every invitation I got. They were so kind, helpful and CALM. The children were dealing with their isolation with such maturity. I respected them, the children and their mothers.

I was touched by their composure and camaraderie. My eyes welled up, and I prayed, "God, please keep these families safe." There I was, again, turning to God.

A spring drizzle fills the air with the smell of wet soil and obliterates the stink of the family shit. The pink of the bougainvillea pops. The weeds cascading from a tree near my window sway like green curtains. A frog has awoken to the crackle of thunder and is announcing his presence with a croak. The birds, that had gone silent and fluffed up like cotton balls in the trees, are shaking the wetness off their wings. I let go of my thoughts, and retreat to the paradise of small things.

Day 5

25 March 2020

The Tokyo Olympic Games are postponed to the spring of 2021. The virus is spreading in Africa: schools in Kenya have shut down. The New York Governor has declared that the rate of the spread of the virus is worse than was feared.

My husband is sitting at home without work. As an actor, his profession is likely to be the last to revive after the scourge begins to subside. When my brother and I were young, my parents used to throw cash at us like bones to the dogs, to keep us out of their hair. But now, when I could really do with financial help, I'm not tossed a five rupee coin. My friend Rupa called from Mumbai yesterday, worried about how she was going to run her house and care for her parents—she's single and lives with them. "Join the group," I said. It is estimated that 94% of the workforce will be impacted by the lockdown. "We can all be poor together."

The already poor will be hardest hit—street vendors, florists, parking attendants, rickshaw pullers and chai shop owners, to name a few. Worst off will be the daily wage earners. The government has to get its act together and deliver food to these people. Direct transfer of money can only work if they have bank accounts, which most of them don't. Sitting here, ruminating on the plight of the poor, besides having to feed, discipline, educate and reassure my own two, high-energy pubescent boys, is more than I can handle. Diversion is the only way to deal with it. So I divert my attention to the peacocks calling.

State borders have been sealed for everything but the essentials. Bhikam Singh has gone off to his village: I have to buy the supplies myself. Donning a mask, scarf, surgical gloves, track pants and trainers, I get into my Mitsubishi Outlander and drive out of the farm. My wheels squishing leaves fallen in the rain, I head to the general store, 15 minutes from home. I come across four other vehicles, not counting the police jeeps patrolling the roads and stationed at the street corners. On a deserted bylane, I see the words "Pratik weds Ankita" written on a faded pink signboard, oddly reminding me of normalcy.

The salesman asks me from behind his mask how he can be of assistance to me. He's friendly and helpful, as if nothing is out of the ordinary. The staff at the chemist too is cool and collected. People in this country have strong faith in karma. Most believe that if they contract the virus, in spite of taking adequate precautions, it was meant to be. Destiny. Even animals have it. And I think of them as I drive back to the farm. If humans are going to have a hard time feeding themselves, how will they feed their pets and livestock? How will the zoo and work animals get fed? People are already throwing out their dogs and cats, fearing they'll get the virus from them. I am bothered by these musings as I drive along familiar roads that were usually teeming with people, dogs, cows and transport vehicles but that now looked like the streets from *The Walking Dead*. My husband and I had binge-watched five seasons of the macabre series just before the advent of the virus. It appears that survival, like in the series, is becoming the sole driving force.

The general stores in the neighbourhood have run out of bread. I stop at the village near my house and stand amongst a band of poor villagers gathered outside a small shop, to get my hands on two loaves. Returning home, I remove my clothes and put them in a bucket to soak in hot water with Dettol. I take a warm bath, and then wipe down every packet and carton I bought with hand sanitiser. At 3.30, I have my lunch.

I was making coffee in the kitchen when my husband called to ask me how we were doing. He got mad at me when I told him I had ventured out to stock up on supplies. "That's not right, no, you shouldn't have gone out of the farm," Raoul said brusquely. A 21-day nationwide curfew has been declared; precious little is left on the shelves in the grocery stores. Only five people are allowed into a store at a time. I grabbed everything I could get my hands on—spaghetti, cheese, jam, peanut butter, honey, vinegar, mayonnaise, breakfast cereal and cans of preserved foods. "I didn't have a choice, I had to go," I told him. He continued to be adamant, unable to wholly grasp my situation. He had chosen to stay in Mumbai with his parents, leaving the entire responsibility of the children to me. I have to make calculated decisions based on the information I have. Every choice at this uncertain, unprecedented, unpredictable time has its risks; but choices *have* to be made.

Raoul has his own anxieties to deal with, like most people do at this time. For a high-energy man like him, sitting at home, I'm sure, is difficult, and that, too, on the 18th floor of a tall and narrow building.

I'm considering sharing information with my husband on a need-to-know basis.

Day 6

26 March 2020

On a day when three billion people are under lockdown, "Maa Adi Shakti" appeared suddenly on a deserted street, brandishing a sword. When the police arrived to arrest her, she disappeared in a swirl of fierce movements, glints of steel and crimson fabric. It was only when the police resorted to a lathi-charge that the devotees, who had rapidly gathered around the self-proclaimed goddess, dispersed and they managed to cease the female in the centre of the swirling. The incident came as no surprise to me; the Chief Minister of the woman's home state isn't exactly an exemplary figure at this time of crisis. He had presided over a puja in a temple, the same week, with a dozen pandits and a multitude of followers.

Dubious characters with unstable temperaments, everywhere, are taking advantage of the current state of uncertainty: a group of suicide bombers entered a gurudwara in the capital of Afghanistan and killed 25 worshippers; Boko Haram is on a rampage in Chad; a group of policemen were beaten up in Bengaluru for doing their job of enforcing the lockdown. Countries are being forced to release thousands of prisoners because the dread of the virus has become worse than the spread of the virus in prison populations. Panic is spreading in the Indian populace; health professionals are getting assaulted daily by their neighbours. People would realise, if only they applied common sense, that their own presence of mind and the medical community are all that stand between them and the disease. Even on a normal day, common sense is uncommon, but in these extenuating circumstances, it appears to be in frightfully short supply.

Supplies, too, are in short supply. Truck drivers are stopped by the police at the borders between states and often thrashed. Medicines aren't reaching the people who need them the most; diabetics, epileptics, asthmatics, patients with heart conditions and mental illness. The G20 has decided to pump five trillion dollars into the global economy—that's great—but when will things on the ground get organised and moving?

The police stopped my father's car yesterday and sent him back home. Parliament is closed, they reminded him, and that politicians like everyone else have to stay home, especially the retired ones.

My friend on the farm across the street, Natalia, made me speak to her husband on the phone; he's having a hard time accepting the severity of the situation. They need diapers for their one-year-old son and their five-year-old daughter requires pencils and a notebook for drawing and homeschooling. He spends his days walking around the property, exercising in their private gym and watching movies, convinced that everything will soon return to normal. "There's no need to be paranoid," he tells his wife. Natalia is frantic. The things she needs are flying off the supermarket shelves. *Someone* has to go out and get them. I told him about my food run and how to gear up and wash off. I hope my talk didn't scare the daylights out of him.

It rained again last night. I heard that frog, the one I'd heard croak yesterday. I want to find his hiding place and say hello. I'm sure he's a big one, maybe even a toad. His croak is loud and low-pitched: he's an alto—he's definitely not a soprano. Heck, he could even be a she! Food for thought.

Day 7

27 March 2020

What is the meaning of life? Why do we exist? The philosophers of Classical Greece pondered over these questions. Farther back in the BC era, Indian sages pondered over them. Today, we're pondering over them too. When Tolstoy hit midlife, he became disillusioned by "the depravities of modern existence", as Irvine Singer puts it in his book, *Meaning in Life*. He wanted to know how best to live his life. Tolstoy's salvation came from seeing the Russian peasants—how they had "minimal expectation, simplicity of heart, a curtailing of personal arrogance, and spontaneous submission to their lot as human beings", notes Singer. It was by observing how the poor had an "intuitive knowledge of how to live" that the author of *War and Peace* discovered faith.

According to the philosopher, Richard Taylor, meaning comes from doing what is "truly noble and good". Most of us keep searching for experiences that are pleasurable or engaging, but we're capable of much more than that. Intelligence and creativity that enable us to come up with ideals and see them through are what differentiate us from the apes. Helping others brings meaning and satisfaction to our lives, and having meaning in life is important because when we look back at the moment of death on how we lived our lives, we'll be content only if we lived a meaningful life. Who wants to die knowing they lived like a parasite their whole life!

In his book, *Finding Meaning; The Sixth Stage of Grief*, David Kessler, renowned expert on grief, says that we should emerge from a devastating experience not with Post Traumatic Stress but "Post Traumatic Growth". In this time of devastation, what we can do—what we *need* to do—is be kind. As my son Rishi likes to say, "Sharing is caring." We *have* to care. That we didn't care is what brought us here.

I sat beside the placid waters of the pond in the front of the farm and watched ripples spread in rings as a carp rose to the surface for a nibble. A swarm of wasps buzzed around a flowering bush, doing what they've always done, probably for eons. My mother's geese honked, making the pair of wild ducks, who have made the pond their home, rise off the water and fly to the next farm. About 20 years ago, my mother released a young black kite she was gifted by a group of street artists. I hadn't seen him for a long time. He swooped down right before me and perched on a tree and started to preen, twisting his head this way and that, mindful of the slightest movement. I observed a cloud travelling leisurely across the blue overhead, no airplanes to disperse its form or obstruct its course. The wild is going back to the wild.

The government came up with this brilliant plan a few years ago to catch the rhesus monkeys that had become a menace around the Parliament House and release them in the Bhatti mines. Many of the farms in Mehrauli, which is near the Bhatti mines, grow vegetables and fruit-bearing trees. It was like the monkeys had arrived in heaven—for the monkeys—but for us it was as if a swarm of locusts had descended upon the land. They began to eat the fruit we made pickles, jam and pies with, and pillaged the vegetable patches. Watching them playing in the trees, I feel guilty that I'm actually enjoying their company. A baby monkey is hanging from his hind legs from a branch, his arms dangling inches above the ground. He drops and rolls down to the edge of the water.

I watch a monkey eat the red flowers of a bottlebrush tree. I didn't know monkeys ate flowers.

The parrots have multiplied as well and for that too, I'm guilty. Feeling sorry for them, I had bought a bunch of caged parrots when I was younger and released them at the farm. The sun is setting now and groups of them are flying above me, chattering as they go. I wonder what they're saying to each other.

As I walk back to the house, I pass a big male monkey sitting on the wall to my right. When I'd passed him earlier, on the way to the pond, he was picking his toes. Now he's sitting there, holding them with his hands, totally still, his eyes looking at them but also not looking at them. He's there but he's also not there. He's in a state of non-being. I reminded myself of something I used to think of a lot, before I had children, when I had more time to myself: we can learn from animals.

Day 8

28 March 2020

Brazil and Pakistan continue to allow religious congregations. Two Palestinian nationals that attended Friday prayers in Pakistan have returned home with the virus. President Bolsonaro gave in to the church and Imran Khan gave in to the ulema: ritual trumped reason. Migrant workers are returning to their villages in Bihar, Jharkhand, Madhya Pradesh and Chhattisgarh. With no trains or buses to take them home, they have no choice but to walk. Even if they had money to buy food along the way, there are no *dhabas* or canteens open along the highways. A family of five, with three children below the age of five, is making the journey of 400 km on a bicycle. Old people, women, children, parents carrying babies, and young men in groups, are making a mass exodus from the cities, spreading into the villages, furthering the reach of the murderous virus.

The migrants have been advised by the police to camp outside their villages for 14 days before entering, an advice that came too late; many have already reached home, hitchhiking on the odd supply truck along the way. Will the government ensure that the displaced people have food, water and basic provisions? The most humane thing to do, according to me, is to provide the migrants transportation. This would also give officials a chance to ensure that they're tested before they disseminate into their villages. I am not an expert: I can only guess what is the best course of action to be taken. But action *has* to be taken.

While the cities empty out, the wild returns. A video of a rare civet crossing a street in Kerala during the lockdown has gone viral on the Internet.

Natalia's husband gathered the courage today to venture outside the safety of their farmhouse to get the provisions his family needs. From the farm beside us, I heard Lakshmi squeak—she's our other neighbour's pet elephant. Lakshmi's mahout used to bring her over and the children would give her baths and feed her apples. They'd fill water in a bucket and get thrills watching her suck it into her trunk and spray herself, standing as close as possible to her to get sprayed, too. Lakshmi is one of the last pet elephants in Delhi, if not the last. We feel lucky to have her near us.

I've been thinking a lot about Lakshmi. Is she getting enough food? I wonder. Her owner lives in the middle of the city. He's a good man, and a wealthy one at that. He provides for her every need: sugarcane from Punjab, hundreds of tubes of Odomos to keep away the mosquitoes, oil to rub on her forehead. She is a spoiled little elephant. I say "little" because, although she's 42 years old, almost the same age as me, she's small in size compared to Indian elephants. She was brought from Nepal when she was five years old. She's had the same mahout since then and he takes good care of her. But, in these uncertain times, when thousands of trucks carrying supplies are parked at state borders, held back by the police, I can't help but hope that Lakshmi is getting her daily requirement of food.

Today, when I heard her squeak—yes, elephants do squeak—I was reassured. Lakshmi is fine, for now.

I haven't seen my brother and his wife since the debacle in the kitchen. I occasionally sit with my parents in the part of the garden an old servant once named *Hawa Mahal*. The gazebo, consisting of four concrete pillars holding up wooden rafters covered by corrugated fibreglass, is anything but a *mahal*. We play along and call it the *Hawa Mahal* in memory of the servant who worked for us for 25 years and is now gone from this world. My father's driver has stopped coming and my father hasn't driven a car for 30 years; he's flown a plane more recently than he's driven a car.

Sitting in the gazebo like a captain held hostage, he complains about the lockdown, hoping, every day, that it ends. I've made him a new routine on a sheet of paper. The window of time he used to go on his excursion was the only part of his day that needed amendment. There, I wrote, "Proposed Series to Watch: The Crown, House of Cards, Parks and Recreation". Below it, I wrote, "2 Episodes". I put down an hour of reading in the routine. I gave him two books, one on the life of the late Princess Gayatri Devi, and another titled, *Karma Cola*. They could have been a sword and scabbard, for all he cared, a fork and knife, or a kukri and nunchuck. He's struggling, predictably, with the notion of change. We will have to wait and watch how it pans out.

Day 9

29 March 2020

The gardener plucks roses and arranges them in the vase that goes in my room. Every rose has its own distinct smell. Would I have learned that if I hadn't been in lockdown?

After appreciating the roses, I go outside to do yoga under the ancient Peepul beside the swimming pool. The Ficus religiosa, or sacred fig, has religious significance in Buddhism, Hinduism and Jainism. The architect who designed the houses on the property couldn't get himself to cut down the ancient tree; A-Block was built around it.

My eyes are closed and I hear the breeze blowing through the semicircle of tall and small trees in this part of the lawn. It blows through a towering tree at a short distance and then makes the dry leaves of the Peepul above me rustle, before entering the grove of mulberry trees round the bend. A goose honks and a seed drops to the ground with a tap, and a bird, flapping its wings, alights on a branch. I'm listening to nature's symphony.

When I open my eyes, the symphony turns into a multi-sensory experience. The breeze brushes against my skin with its feathery touch while I watch a white butterfly fluttering around a cluster of pink and purple flowers. A parrot sits in a flourish of leaves, bright as emeralds, while the sky curves above us all. I've become like the monkey I saw yesterday on my way back from the pond; I'm in a state of being and also not being. I'm one with the elements.

Buddhist monks tell us to live in the moment. Be mindful, they say, ever aware of what you are doing and where you are, like when you're chewing your food, taking a shower or going for a walk. We humans have become so used to searching for stimulation that we've forgotten the joy of *just being*.

The people in exodus are in a perpetual state of living-in-the-moment—nothing focuses the mind on the present like hunger, thirst and pain. Workers are migrating in waves, leaving Rajasthan, Hyderabad, Maharashtra, returning to their villages in the northern states. Daily wage earners make up 80% of the workforce in India. Out of work, the only course of action to take, they've collectively decided, is to head back home with their meagre belongings.

When I watch these people doing a slow march across the country, carrying their young in their arms or their old on their backs, women balancing loads on their heads while clutching their babies, I can't help but think of my family. The poor, who have nothing, are going through great pains to deliver their loved ones through this humanitarian crisis. No matter how tired, thirsty or hungry they are, they still have love.

Love. It's something in short supply in my family. My parents do their own thing, stockpiling their provisions and sticking to themselves. It's the same with my brother and his family unit. If I fall ill, I'm afraid there will be no volunteers to take care of my children. Each to his own—or her own—that's the motto here. I wonder if this was a by-product of success—if success can be measured by wealth and power alone—or if my folks were always this way; aloof right from the start. Everybody's bothered about who's got what claim over which portion of these ten acres of land. The same is happening everywhere in Delhi's so-called high society; families are fighting battles in court over money and property—this is mine and that is yours.

My paternal grandfather, who became an ascetic midlife, used to say, *"Hum nange aye hain aur hum nange jayenge,"* meaning that we were born naked and we will depart with nothing but our nakedness. People caught up in material delusions have no idea what's coming: the virus is spreading fast and killing without discrimination. There is no silver lining. Families will have to unite. The coming together of families and peoples of different races and faiths, may, in the end, be the only silver lining to this whole fiasco.

Day 10

30 March 2020

The United Kingdom's Prime Minister, Health Minister and heir apparent, Prince Charles, have been diagnosed with the virus. They're receiving treatment in quarantine.

39,545 people have died so far of the mystery disease—so state the official figures.

America, the richest nation in the world, has run out of ventilators. They're converting car-manufacturing units into ventilator-manufacturing units. In India, a sugar factory is making hand sanitisers. Nurses are catching the disease every day from their patients. Army men are contracting the disease while patrolling sensitive zones. Millions are going without food. We've become the caged animals now, locked in our homes, our hearts breaking from witnessing so much death.

In our pursuit of fun and leisure, we had put the entire burden of saving the world on the selfless. The pandemic is forcing us to tap into our humanity; some of us will have to die, sadly, for others of us to learn that we *have* to care for our planet and what happens to our fellow beings.

Gloves, masks and antiseptic solutions have become near impossible to get. I gave the last four masks I had to the guard posted at the gate. I also gave him the two pairs of surgical gloves I had managed to buy before everything ran out in the stores. His job is to make sure that any staff member heading outside for supplies puts these on before leaving the farm. The protective gear is to be returned to the guard when they return. He is to wash the masks and gloves in a mug of hot water with three caps of Dettol (my last bottle) after every use. Once sterilised, they are to be hung up to dry in the sun. It's the best I can do to safeguard the people living at the farm, which has, in a way, become a village of its own. I've taken it upon myself to protect it the best I can.

In this village, there are 14 children.

Day 11

31 March 2020

Tablighi Jamaat. It means "a group of preachers". 8,400 people attended an event in Delhi organised by this group, many of whom arrived just days before international flights were cancelled. They came in from Thailand, Philippines and Malaysia, hotspots of the virus.

Ignoring the Prime Minister's call for social distancing and obeying the commands given by the head of the Jamaat, 3,000 attendees set up camp inside the organisation's Markaz building in Nizamuddin. The foreign nationals, who were supposed to declare their travel history to the authorities but didn't do so, were hosted by local families and religious organisations. After the Jamaat refused to stop the sermons and disperse the crowds, evacuation of the Markaz was started two days ago, on 29 March. 441 of the evacuees are showing symptoms of the virus. The infected have been hospitalised and 1,600 are quarantined. Ten are dead. Of the 24 new cases in New Delhi today, 18 had attended the Markaz. But that is not the worse part.

By the time the Markaz was evacuated, hundreds of pilgrims had already returned home, spreading to 20 states across the subcontinent. The 400 that are untraceable are being referred to as "super spreaders". Authorities are presently engaged in the monumental task of tracing their whereabouts and identifying those who may have come into contact with them. Aside from the labour migration and consequent crowding at the Delhi border, this is the single most devastating event in the war against the virus right now. Add to this the fact that we're testing nowhere near as much as we should be. The UK tested 1,788 people per million and what a mess that got them into!—more people are dying there than can be accounted for. South Korea, in comparison, conducted 7,622 tests per million and in doing so managed to flatten the curve on the virus. Germany too used extensive testing to stop a rise in cases. India is currently testing 20 samples per million.

There's a reason why Japan has relatively been spared by the disease. The Japanese have always had a high level of personal hygiene. I remember when I was in Tokyo for my honeymoon— nearly two decades ago—the taxi driver was wearing a mask and gloves. The Japanese eat with chopsticks while Indians eat with their hands. Washing hands before and after meals or using the toilet is, regrettably, not practiced as extensively as it should be here, mainly because of people's limited access to soap and water. Typhoid, a bacterial infection passed through contaminated food and water, is still common in our country. The current virus, like Typhoid, can stay alive in faeces for days and can be spread by way of infrequent handwashing. People will have to get more vigilant about maintaining hygiene—a whole lot more vigilant.

My worst fear has come to be—India has entered Phase 3 of the spread of the virus and Mumbai has become its epicentre. Three localities in the city have been sealed.

Containment. Will India be able to do it, with its high population, low hygiene levels and resistance to social distancing?

Day 12

1 April 2020

When we got married, Raoul insisted that his parents run the house. If his mother wouldn't get to run the house, he asserted, she would become depressed. I had witnessed her panic attacks before—lying on the carpet, breathless, a servant rubbing her feet, and at times, having to be taken to the hospital and administered oxygen. My husband assured me that when our children came into the picture, the arrangement would allow me the freedom to give them my undivided attention, which, in view of my own childhood, didn't sound like a bad idea to me.

That it was an idea that nearly undid my marriage and gave me over a decade of pain is not the point here. There was a history to my mother-in-law's insecurity. Just like my history led me to accept, voluntarily, my own subjugation, her history made her anxious about the future. My husband is a Kashmiri Pandit and belongs to one of the thousands of families that were forced by militancy to leave their ancestral homes and migrate to other parts of the country. He landed in Mumbai as a 17 year old, with a beaten suitcase and a tiger's spirit. He braved it out, and after enduring untold struggles, managed to make enough money to bring his parents and sister over from Jammu.

One day, when my mother-in-law wasn't home and I needed something from the storeroom for my baby, I opened it to find it was crammed with supplies. *I'm kept on such a tight budget*, I thought, *while there are enough supplies in here to get us through a siege!* There were sacks of rice and wheat, every kind of dal available in the market, crates of Pepsi, cases of mineral water, kitchen rolls, biscuits, bottles of sunflower and mustard oil, toilet cleaners, mosquito repellents, boxes of washing powder, soap and toothpaste. My in-laws had three refrigerators, one in every room, filled with zip-lock packets bulging with raisins, almonds, pistachios, peanuts, walnuts, syrups and spices.

Bundles of clothes that no one wore anymore sat on top of our cupboards. The hoarded things represented my mother-in-law's invisible scars, the ones she had on the inside. They signified the wounds that being robbed of all she possessed had inflicted on her—of her things, of her identity, of her sense of security. Possession: it had become a necessity. To possess her son, to possess objects, items, and certainty of the future.

Last night, before I slept, I happened to glance at the poem by Swami Vivekananda on the wall beside my bed. I had stuck it there alongside other interesting and inspiring material I'd cut out of magazines when I was young. Some of the pages are fading and curling at the corners. The poem reads:

Kali, The Mother

The stars are blotted out,
The clouds are covering clouds,

It is darkness vibrant, sonant.
In the roaring, whirling wind
Are the souls of a million lunatics
Just loose from the prison-house,
Wrenching trees by the roots,
Sweeping all from the path...
The sea has joined the fray,
And swirls up mountain-waves,
To reach the pitchy sky.
The flash of lurid light
Reveals on every side
A thousand, thousand shades,
Of Death begrimed and black—
Scattering plagues and sorrows,
Dancing mad with joy,
Come, Mother, come!
For Terror is Thy name,
Death is in Thy breath,
And every shaking step
Destroys a world for e'er.
Thou "Time", the All-Destroyer!
Come, O Mother, come!
 Who dares misery love,
And hugs the form of Death,
Dances in Destruction's dance,
To him the Mother comes.

I'm going to attempt to translate the poem.

I'll start with "Thou 'Time', the All-Destroyer!" Kal means time. Kali is the feminine of time. Vivekananda calls time the All-Destroyer because destruction is essential for creation: death makes way for life. He says, "Death is in Thy breath", to Kali because as the All-Destroyer, she is the bringer of the end. The association of death and breath is obvious; it is when a body releases its last breath that it dies. To think of one's own death is terrifying for most people, and so the poet says, "Terror is Thy name". By using the word plague, he means disease, and by the word sorrow, he means hunger, famine and war—the bringers of death. It's interesting that he says Kali is "Dancing mad with joy" when she's "Scattering plagues and sorrows".

What he means, in my interpretation, is that the act of destroying is just as joyful as the act of creating. This relates to the Buddhist and Vedic teachings that advise us to view pleasure and pain with equanimity. Vivekananda is alluding to eras of history when he says, "Every shaking step Destroys a world for e'er". The world is never the same following a global calamity; it wasn't the same after the Crusades; it wasn't the same after the devastation caused by World Word II; and it won't be the same after this virus is done with its destruction. "Come, O Mother, come"! Why would we invite the destroyer of worlds? We invite her because without the lessons that destruction teaches us, we cannot, or will not, change our ways—the ways that lead us to calamity in the first place. Why would we hug "the form of Death" and "dance in Destruction's dance"?

By accepting the misery that befalls us, by submitting to it, even embracing it, we surrender our will to the will of time. The one who surrenders to the unknown conquers the fear of the unknown. In conquering fear, we open ourselves to infinite bliss, to the supreme. Kali comes to the heroes and heroines who have conquered fear. It is to them she reveals the meaning of life.

The eastern scriptures tell us to view pleasure and pain equally. Practicing equanimity through good and bad times helps us maintain equilibrium when confronted with real horrors, like famine, drought, war and disease. Maintaining equilibrium is the only way to get through the tough times and come out the other side—not broken, but wiser. As David Kessler, the grief expert, says, recover from a grievous event not with Post Traumatic Stress but "Post Traumatic Growth". That's the same message Swami Vivekananda is trying to give us through his poem on Kali.

Day 13

2 April 2020

352 people from the Markaz have tested positive for the virus. A man who returned to his home in Mumbai from Nizamuddin has died of the disease, but not before creating a cluster in Asia's largest slum, Dharavi.

Wheat, potatoes, papayas, oranges, grapes and watermelons are ready for harvesting but there are no workers to cut them or buyers to buy them. Crops are rotting in the fields. Lakhs of trucks are stranded on borders between states. The supply chain has choked up. The farmers are suffering. Their suffering has just begun.

Health workers everywhere continue to be heckled, stoned and spat at. The level of ignorance in this country will enable the virus to kill countless more than would die otherwise. While most of us are hunkered down in our homes, the mindless and thoughtless, with the firm and baseless belief that God will save them, go about attending religious gatherings, roaming the bylanes and engaging in hooliganism.

My children left the door to the dining room open and a monkey came inside and stole the bananas on the table.

I baked a banana-walnut cake today—before the monkey got in and stole the remaining bananas. Spring Break has ended and homeschooling has begun; a new and challenging experience for the boys. I don't know how much they'll learn from this improvised method, but their education is not my top priority right now; their health and safety are.

It isn't unusual for me to have erotic thoughts about my husband when I'm away from him, but in the two weeks I've been here, I haven't had a glimmer of arousal. Watching the mounting death toll on the news, the rapid spread of the disease and no solution in sight, is the surest way to make the fiercest of libidos frigid. I'm trying not to let these awful developments shrivel my soul. Maintain equilibrium, I tell myself.

I heard the toad croak, again, today. Or frog. Don't know which he is. Or she. Or it. I peered into the vegetation outside my room from where I've heard him, once or twice a day since the first rain. He's so well camouflaged that I can't spot him, no matter how hard I look.

Day 14

3 April 2020

I get a kick out of seeing my parents spending time with their grandchildren. They have no choice but to do it: they're literally forbidden from going anywhere or meeting anyone. The pandemic is giving us no choice but to look inward. Maybe we really needed that—to be blocked from external stimuli and look inside—inside our hearts, inside our homes, into our relationships.

My friends are fretting over how they are going to get through the next few months, sitting at home, with little to do. I'm reading a book on Vedanta. According to this school of philosophy, happiness and bliss don't come from the outside. The material world can only give us a limited amount of pleasure, for the objects that bring us joy are the same that bring us pain. To find bliss, we have to turn inward; we have to control the wavering mind and go beyond pleasure, misery and fear. This can only be done by observing the mind at all times. When we see a negative thought arise, we must rein it in and introduce a different, positive thought. By thus controlling the mind, we can go beyond it and get to what we really are—spirit.

The best way to discipline the mind, Vedanta suggests, is by concentration. Find an activity and focus your mind on it, be it reading, writing, sewing, cooking, playing a musical instrument, ironing or solving puzzles. In extreme situations, like the one we're in, we can start with the simple things. We can choose a potted plant in the kitchen and concentrate on its wellness; care for it; will it to grow. Expanding, then, to the more complex organisms, we can do the same for the people we've hunkered down with; make a conscious decision to engage with them positively. Concentration is the means by which we can get the mind to obey us. When the mind is trained, we're able to go beyond it, to the spirit, which is the same spirit that pervades the universe; we experience the state that transcends the mind—bliss.

I've started sewing masks for everyone at the farm, from its youngest resident to its eldest. I found some cotton fabric left from the days I used to get my clothes stitched by a tailor. Each mask will have four layers of fabric for the rectangular part that covers the nose and mouth. Of the fabric I have, I can make 25 masks.

So far, I've made five.

Day 15

4 April 2020

60,000 people have died of the virus, globally. One death takes place every three minutes in New York. So desperate is the need for beds, a hospital has spilled into Central Park.

38% of the cases of the virus are in people 70 years and older. That explains why Italy has the highest rate of mortality: the country's average age is 47. Add to this the fact that 23% of its citizens are 65 or older. Figures notwithstanding, fitness factors—more than the age factor—determine how the virus plays out in an individual; a healthy 60-year-old can survive it while a 40-year-old patient with pre-existing medical conditions or a weaker immune system can succumb to it.

Scientists speculate that if a vaccine isn't developed in the next six months, two-thirds of the population of the world could end up contracting the disease. It is safe to say, going by the statistics on the behaviour and mortality rate of the virus, that the young will inherit the earth. The year 2020 has felt like a horror film, so far, but it's turning out to be more of a science fiction movie. The youth demonstrating on the parks and streets, begging us, scolding us, demanding that we change our greedy, complacent ways, may, literally, become our future leaders. We could soon be a civilisation led by people like Malala Yousafzai, Greta Thunberg, Jamie Margolin of Zero Hour, David Hogg and Emma Gonzalez, survivors of the shooting at the high school in Parkland, Florida, and Xiuhtezcatl Roske-Martinez, the 15-year-old who spoke at the United Nations on the inability of world leaders to take action on the crisis facing the earth. Martinez is the boy who famously said, "What's at stake right now is the existence of my generation." Uncannily, the disease is sparing his generation. Could it be so that he and others like him can lead humanity to a better tomorrow? The youth are the innocent victims we brought into a world of our creation, a world that is choking, shrinking, melting and burning. And when they tried to have a say in the matter, we didn't listen to them. Fate may force us to take a back seat so that they can lead the way. Such an eventuality may not just be the imagination of an over-active middle-aged mind working under lockdown. We, the old, are resistant to change. The minds of the young are open, malleable—they can bring the change we need. Their governance may be the best way—the *only* way—forward.

I envisage the world going back to a more natural state under the leadership of the young. We'd be through with grabbing; we'd build on what we've already built. Wildlife has a right over half the planet, something we've collectively, and conveniently, forgotten. The wilderness used to cover 65% of the earth in the 1930s. It now covers 25%. The young understand that we can't afford to lose anymore; further degradation of the wilderness will throw off the balance of the earth's ecosystem. Earth matters. It is all that matters. We've grabbed enough already. Enough—that would be the clarion call of the new world order. I can see us making the best of what we have, perfecting it, building gardens on top of skyscrapers and bridges to connect them; making entire townships in the sky. Trains running through forests would run on elevated tracks so as not to obstruct ancient wildlife corridors. We'd go electric and fly automobiles rather than drive them on tarmac. We'd go upwards for living, farming, for every aspect of our existence, rather than outward. Living would become an art.

The image of an ambulance is projected on the Empire State building to give thanks to the overworked emergency workers of New York. This is our present, a present of our own design. The pandemic is giving us a chance to make things right. Let's take it, reconfigure our future; allow the youth to lead.

Day 16

5 April 2020

A correspondent on the news last night did a report on the first drive-in testing facility started by Dr Dang in Punjab. Referring to the people coming through it, he said, "The suspect stays in the car as he is tested." Anyone with a fever and cough feels like a suspect, to be hunted and quarantined, branded and stigmatised. I've been working on my masks at break-neck speed, doing the best I can to ensure that no one from this farm becomes the next suspect.

Domestic abuse, like the virus, has increased exponentially. I was afraid this would happen as a result of stricter lockdowns being enforced across the globe. Again, me the pessimist, thinking about what could happen between discordant couples living in isolation. Patriarchs, who should be caring and providing for their wards, any which way they can, are crumbling under the financial and emotional pressure the pandemic is exerting on them. Violence against women, and the children who have to bear witness to it, or are at the receiving end of it, cannot be helped under the circumstances: rescue centres are either full or closed. Phone calls by women to helplines, globally, have reached an unprecedented volume. In India, cases of sexual abuse of children have doubled. A United Nations spokesperson came on television and expressed his concern over the rise in incidents of domestic abuse.

Here's a poem I've written on behalf of all the women locked down with abusive men:

> *You are no one to call me mad*
> *You are no one to call me a bitch*
> *You are no one to pity me*
> *You are no one to tell me I'm useless*
> *You are no one to stop me*
> *For you were once someone dear to me*
> *Who has now become no one to me.*

Gorging on grisly movies, my husband is dealing with this apocalypse with enviable calm. I lament to him on the phone about people going hungry, farmers committing suicide, teenagers and toddlers under house arrest, abandoned pets and patients on ventilators. I tell him how I have to take in a deep breath when I turn on the black box in my room to learn of the developments of each new and harrowing day. He tells me, "Accept what's happening or you'll drive yourself crazy." He says, "Those who have to go will go and those who are destined to stay will stay." It's a stoic view to take but it's what gets him through the day. The doctrine of karma provides a metaphysical lens through which to view the events that are happening to us and around us. It puts them in a larger context, and by doing so, aids us in making sense of them. When I feel overwhelmed, bombarded each day with the death and destruction this pestilence is bringing upon us, I try to console myself by saying, "It's for some larger design you can't understand, yet," and stay sane.

Day 17

6 April 2020

The wind gives movement to the trees and sends flowers on invisible wings to alight on the grass. The Peepul tree, bare a week ago, has birthed a profusion of leaves, pinkish-yellow in infancy, impatient to grow to maturity. The rambling rose bush on the rafters outside my room is in full bloom. Hoverflies keep still their delicate wings as they draw nectar from the sunburst centres of the wild pink roses. A yellow hummingbird couple chases each other around the bushes, playing, like the monkeys play in the trees. A single blue butterfly flutters across the pink clusters in their leafy beds. The natural world looks happy: only we humans are caught in a wretched web of our own making.

The labyrinthine walls separating the three houses and portioning the land are the dominion of the monkeys. Their limbs lazily dangling from the wall, the adults take a siesta in the afternoon, while their babies use them as an obstacle course to jump over as they run along the ramparts. I see a female plucking ticks off the back of a giant male with a red behind. Popping them in her mouth, she munches on the nutritious tit-bits. I've been watching the monkeys so much these days that I'm afraid I'll end up going monkey-mad.

I've been trying to train my own two monkeys to lift the toilet seat; it exasperates me to no end to discover telltale yellow droplets on the seat when I go into the washroom after them. I've reached the conclusion that it's easier to train monkeys than boys.

There's one creature, though, more difficult to train than both monkeys and the boys—Whitey. She's my new and, admittedly, irritating companion. She's also the most disposable creature in the current state of affairs—a stray dog. With no food stalls open to eat scraps from, street animals, like humans, are suffering during the pandemic. Whitey was a puppy when she snuck into our farm a little less than a year ago. My mother didn't have the heart to throw her out, and so she stayed. The same goes for Blackey and Nilli. Blackey got the name Blackey because she's black. Whitey was named Whitey because she's white. Nilli is Nilli because her eyes are blue. We also have Harsil, who's a Tibetan mastiff, and Guddi, a poodle.

Whitey, at some indeterminate point, decided I was her favourite human. She cries and scratches the paint off my door until I let her into my room. Once inside, she'll jump on me, force me to pet her, fall to the ground, kick her legs in glee, and then wail to go outside again. Not long after, she'll return and repeat the routine. She's torn a sofa in the living room, chewed a leg off the dining table and stolen several shoes, including shoes belonging to staff members from outside their quarters. Since she's with me most of the time, I've taken it upon myself to train her. I've managed to stop her from chewing the furniture and got her to understand the meaning of the word "No", though, I admit, it took some spanking to teach her. I gave her a bath yesterday and was surprised at how strong a medium-sized female stray dog can be; she struggled and strained against me like a wild pig at the slaughterhouse.

Today, my older son asked me what the word "horny" meant. The boys are growing up.

Day 18

7 April 2020

The moon was a white disc, bobbing in an ocean of blackness, before clouds rumbled in and threw silver streaks across the sky. When the storm blew over, and everything became still again, fireflies sprinkled the lawn and twinkled. My brother and I used to call them "butt burners" when we were small. One entered my room and twinkled for me all night.

The leaves of the poolside Peepul are bigger and greener this morning. Two monkeys are sitting on the wall, holding hands, like humans. Why am I seeing so many two's—two ducks, two kingfishers, two hummingbirds and two monkeys holding hands? Could it be because I'm missing my partner? It's springtime—the time for love. Everybody in the garden is out in twos, everybody, but me.

My husband says he wants to steal a bicycle and ride it to Delhi to be with me. He's finished watching the final season of *The Walking Dead*, wherein the main antagonist goes around smashing people's brains out with a baseball bat wrapped in barbed wire, that he fondly calls Lucille. Today, he forwarded me the trailer of *Train to Busan 2*, another zombie movie. All hell's broken loose and the man wants to watch people oozing puss, spitting blood, growing warts and gorging on human flesh! I guess everyone has his or her own way of getting through this existential crisis; Raoul's is watching movies till 6:00 am and waking up at 2. 30 p.m. To be fair, I used to binge-watch with him into the wee hours of the next day, on most Saturday nights. I don't have Netflix here and I have to make sure the kids get up early for their online homeschooling. I'm in bed by 12, at the latest.

Raoul spot-exercises every day on our balcony and reads for an hour, and I'm guessing, or hoping, fills his day with other wholesome activities, such as playing with the dog and enjoying the company of our three rescue cats. I pray he maintains his equilibrium throughout; we could be facing many lockdowns up ahead, until this scourge is properly managed. Maintaining equilibrium is key, for all of us.

Day 19

8 April 2020

Morgues in New York have stopped accepting bodies; there are so many coming in that they have to be stacked up against the walls. To make more space for the corpses, lines of 18-tyre trailer trucks are parked outside hospitals. Parks are being converted into cemeteries, dug up to accommodate the dead deprived of a funeral service, or a final farewell from their loved ones, before entering the arms of the earth.

I got a call from my friend Rupa. She's worried. Her sister lives in New York with her husband and their two-year-old son and six-month-old daughter. Rupa's family is vegetarian. She has a rescue dog named Oreo, a Dalmatian, who she treats like a son. She has a low-pitched voice and a gentle demeanour—I've never known her to be an angry person. Today, I was clearly not speaking to the same Rupa. "Why does my sister have to suffer for the sins others have committed?" she said harshly. "She's never eaten veal or stolen from the poor. She isn't a deserter. Do you know that Americans abandon millions of dogs every year? They abandon their pets. They abandon their old. They separate children from their mothers and put them in cages at the border. Who do they think they are! They meddle in the affairs of other nations for self-gain. They create wars in remote countries, and then, after destroying the place, pretend they're helping to keep the peace. Maybe that's why they have a liar and a hypocrite as a president." I stopped her there. "Rupa," I said, "bitterness isn't going to get you anywhere." I gave her the spiel I've been giving all my friends, about the importance of meditation, exercise, reading, making a routine and following it. But my words sounded hollow, even to me, because I, too, was disappointed in the United States. I'm a wildlife enthusiast, and the fact that there are more captive tigers in America than roaming the forests of the Indian subcontinent bothers me. In America, if you've got the money, you can buy anything you want; exotic animals, guns, lots and lots of guns: you can buy whatever and whoever you please. Money makes America tick. And yet, despite being the richest country in the world, it can't hide its social inequities and lack of will to remedy them. That 60% of the people dying in hospitals across New York are Blacks and Hispanics is proof. The minorities were disadvantaged right from the start, shafted by a poor healthcare system and systemic racism. The high frequency of animal cruelty, spousal abuse, racism and classism is indicative of the nation's weak moral fabric. Before this epoch-changing event befell us, we all, not just the Americans, were getting morally bankrupt.

The International Monetary Fund has called the impact of the pandemic "the worst economic crisis since the Great Depression". They've said that the virus will cause widespread unemployment in America. I shudder to think of what it'll do to India; indeed, of what it's already doing. I'm grateful to be behind these walls so I don't have to see it first-hand; the helplessness I'd feel would shatter my equilibrium. I'm too broke to help anyone. Maintaining equilibrium is the only way I can get myself and my children through this, alive.

The pandemic has brought a pause; it has stopped everything in its tracks. When the planet was screaming for help, we weren't decisive; we didn't act; we didn't implement the changes that were required. The pause is twisting humanity's arm backwards, now, forcing us to do a re-think. When the pause button lifts, we will *have* to go in for an overhaul. And if we don't, the youth will see to it that we do—one way or another. They aren't going to forgive us for this. We don't deserve forgiveness either. We've really messed up.

Day 20

9 April 2020

Ninety seven people have died of the virus in Mumbai. The cases in the city have risen to 876. The most dangerous cluster is in Dharavi. The government is trying to achieve cluster containment—it's when an entire neighbourhood is sealed—but in a colony with one toilet for every 1,400 residents, curbing the spread will be nothing short of a miracle. When a colony is sealed, food and other necessities are delivered to residents' doorsteps. They're provided with a helpline; if someone needs urgent medical attention, they can call for assistance. Medical attention: this is why people need to value medics and not harass them! Two doctors, yet again, were attacked by their neighbours while returning home from their shift at the Safdarjung Hospital in New Delhi.

Three astronauts have lifted off to the International Space Station, 250 miles above sea level (the safest place to be under earthly circumstances!). Anyone complaining about living in isolation for too long should remember them, hovering up there for close to six months in vast emptiness.

I'm relieved that my father has settled into his homebound routine, as the lockdown is likely to be extended by another two weeks. It can go on for even longer. My parents have started watching *The Crown*. Dad likes it, but not enough to get his mind off wine. He's been asking around for a bottle. He's not supposed to be drinking; his doctors have told him: one glass on his birthday and one to celebrate the New Year is all he's allowed. So much for that! My brother— the only one who's got liquor on the property—ended up succumbing to dad's persuasions and giving him a bottle of his finest red.

My aunt who lives in the third house, C-Block, got a cancerous growth removed from her body one hour before hospitals stopped conducting emergency surgeries. She's back home, recovering from the operation. I attempted to visit her today but she's afraid of getting an infection. I've sent her a recipe for an Ayurvedic immunity-boosting tonic. I hope she takes it regularly, till she's better.

Lakshmi's not allowed to have visitors even if she wanted them. I had our gardener pop over to her farm to see how she's doing. He was promptly returned. No one's allowed in. The elephant was in the habit of taking a walk around the neighbourhood every day. She must really be missing her walks.

My son Robin discovered a cycle rickshaw in the weeds at the back of the property. As it turns out, it belonged to the trust my mother founded to benefit street artists. The kids have been taking turns to ride the rickshaw around the farm and take each other for rides on it. Its tyres are totally flat. I'll have to wait till the lockdown lifts to get new ones. Robin took me for a ride on the doddering contraption. The ride was wobbly, to say the least, but fun.

The lockdown rules have become stricter; there are police check posts at every 5 km in every direction. No one's allowed any further. Persons seen without masks are liable to be struck by a policeman's *lathi*.

I've made ten masks and distributed them to the staff and their kin. No one from this farm is going to get whacked by a *lathi*!

Day 21

10 April 2020

Thousands of migrants took to the streets in a diamond district in Gujarat, to demonstrate against joblessness and hunger. They pelted stones and torched cars.

Chief Ministers are rising to the challenge of safeguarding their states. Working with slow bureaucratic machinery and inadequate resources, they're showing grit and determination in their effort to curb the spread of the disease.

While the rest of the world is in the throes of the virus that began in Wuhan, the Chinese have resumed slaughtering wild animals for their meat. The Wuhan market is open for business, as are several more like it, across the country. 100,000 people have died globally. In some countries, the havoc of the virus has only just begun. But that hasn't stopped the Chinese from going back to farming tigers like crops, slaughtering them and soaking their bones in alcohol to make traditional medicines. They've gone back to hunting bears in the wild or breeding them, using the cruellest of methods to extract bile from their bodies. They're stealing pangolins from their habitats in Africa. They are buying the horns of poached rhinos and grinding them into remedial powders that have no efficacy. It's all there in these markets. How much suffering and death are we willing to tolerate before we put an end to the savagery? When the world is on a stronger wicket—when the dying is done—are we going to shut these markets down once and for all, or not? If we're going to look the other way, after having gone through all this, we should brace ourselves for another, and possibly deadlier, pandemic. The next one will send us back to the caves. That's where we'll have to start all over again. Reset.

Day 22

11 April 2020

"Thou art That." What the Upanishads mean by this is that the spirit that resides in you is the same as the spirit that resides in all living organisms. Indeed, it is the spirit that resides in the entire universe. It means that you are the same as the one you love or torture: you are the bear that you are tormenting or the fox that you are skinning alive. There's nothing that distinguishes you from them but their form. "Our separation from each other is an optical illusion," said Albert Einstein. As a statement, "Thou art That" aligns with the concept of karma, which holds that if you wrong any other living organism, you, in turn, will be wronged in equal measure. The law of karma proposes the exact same hypothesis as Newton's law—for every action, there's an equal and opposite reaction—and, therefore, may be viewed as scientific. It means, quite literally, that you will become the bear that you torture for its bile or the fox that you skin alive, in some future life. It is inevitable.

The belief in reincarnation is shared by practitioners of Buddhism, Hinduism, Sikhism, Jainism and Taoism. Socrates, Pythagoras and Plato also believed in it. They even taught about it. Pythagoras claimed that he remembered his past lives. The third century biblical scholar, Origen, pointed out the passages in the Bible that indicate that Jesus was aware of reincarnation. In regards to Elias from the Old Testament, Jesus tells his followers in the Gospel of St. Matthew that the man, Elias, had returned as John the Baptist. Even Christ's rising from the dead, I believe, in some remote way, endorses the idea of everlasting existence. In 553 AD, the Byzantine emperor, Justinian, ordered the removal of references to reincarnation and the immortality of the soul from ancient church writings and editions of the Bible. Why he decided to do it remains a mystery to modern-day scholars. *The Zohar*, a text from the Cabala of Judaism, too, makes references to past and future lives. There's a verse even in the Koran that refers to reincarnation. It says, "And you were dead, and He brought you back to life. And He shall cause you to die, and shall bring you back to life, and in the end shall gather you unto Himself."

The Sufi poet, Rumi, reflects on reincarnation in the following poem:

I died as a mineral and became a plant,
I died as plant and rose to animal,
I died as animal and I was Man.
Why should I fear? When was I less by dying?

Napoleon used to tell his troops that he was Charlemagne in a previous life. Benjamin Franklin wrote, "Finding myself to exist in the world, I believe I shall, in some shape or other, always exist."

The British poet laureate, John Masefield, succinctly and beautifully stated his belief in reincarnation in the following poem:

I hold that when a person dies
His soul returns again to earth;
Arrayed in some new flesh-disguise
Another mother gives him birth.
With sturdier limbs and brighter brain
The old soul takes the road again.

There must be something to the doctrine of karma—something that appeals to the logical mind. Or else why would so many religions and figures from history, literature, science and philosophy refer to it? Why would the majority of earth's population live by it? In its most rudimentary form, it means, "Do unto others as you would have them do unto you," the Golden Rule based on the words of Jesus in the Sermon on the Mount. The Golden Rule appears in Judaism, Taoism, Zoroastrianism, Buddhism, Christianity, Hinduism, and other less-known religions. It was endorsed in the 1993 "Declaration Toward a Global Ethic" by leaders of all faiths. Shouldn't that be incentive enough to stop wronging? Our actions *do* have consequences, and that is why spiritual luminaries and world religions impress upon us to be mindful of our actions, and do unto others *only* that we would have them do unto us.

Day 23

12 April 2020

Their pick-up truck crashing into a police barricade, members of the Nihang sect of Sikhism brazenly defied the curfew in Patiala. Blue robes bellowing, they jumped out of the vehicle and fought the police, one striking a policeman on the wrist with a sword and severing his hand. The appendage fell to the ground, and another policeman—the only one with the presence of mind after witnessing the shocking act of violence—picked it up and wrapped it in cloth. Holding his hand against his chest like the precious object it was, the assaulted officer was bundled into a van and rushed to the hospital. After a seven-hour surgery, the hand was attached back to the wrist. Doctors are not sure how well it will function after the wound heals.

After the grisly news report, came another, about an earthquake in New Delhi, a 3.4 on the Richter scale. The quake was followed by a series of tremors, which still continue. If the earthquakes escalate, it will spell more trouble and grief for the capital's residents and further encumber its government, which is overwhelmed by the pandemic to the point of incapacitation. I clicked past channels on the TV until I came upon a video of a group of doctors dancing; it had gone viral on TikTok. It was refreshing to see the doctors and nurses, in their protective gear, dancing gaily. It's a cliché, but there's a reason clichés exist; the nurses and doctors really *are* the heroes in this pandemic.

I sometimes see the black kite gifted to my mom by the street artists, up in the sky, making languid loops. He's actually more brown than black. When he flies low, I can make out his feathers and the curved beak in his small head, but when he's up high, I only know that it's him. At times, he's with a partner. But mostly, he's on his own—the one lord of the sky above Dera Mandi Road. I imagine the kites looking down at the hungry hordes gathered in camps and on train tracks just as I see them on television. Gliding on the currents of air, they watch a man scooping spilled milk from the road and into a mug, while dogs lap at it downstream, baffled by what they're seeing. In rural districts, kites look upon fields of wheat, ready for harvesting and no one in sight to do the cutting. They swoop down to eat the rodents feeding on unattended mounds of rotting fruit. One's loss is another's gain. For humans, the loss is far too much. The gain is of the wild.

Flamingos are back on Mumbai's Palm Beach. The endangered Olive Ridley turtles have returned to the beaches of Odisha to lay their eggs.

Day 24

13 April 2020

38 children in Tamil Nadu have tested positive for the virus, an uncommon phenomenon for the disease, since it's been affecting mostly adults or the elderly. The children were likely from poor families and had malnutrition.

My father went for a cat scan this morning. When the doctors checked him out, they said that he had suffered a heart attack three days back, the day the astronauts went into space. He was immediately admitted into the Intensive Care Unit at the Medanta Hospital.

Yesterday, at Sunday lunch, I noticed that he was sweating. He got dizzy when he stood up. I asked him if this was a freak occurrence or some new symptom. He said that he'd been feeling dizzy for some days. His servant later confirmed to me that he was breathless at night: he couldn't make it up the stairs to the dining room; he was taking his dinner in his room. Out on his walk, he felt so dizzy, the servant said, that he lay down on the grass. Distressing as this revelation was to me, I didn't dare bring it up with my mother; no one dares bring anything up with her that she doesn't want to hear. Zip, zilch, nada. Mom's the boss. Mom's the final word. That something so concerning could have happened without my brother and I coming to know of it shows the separateness of these houses—and the separateness of its occupants. There are secrets, here, that only the Man Friday knows.

The Arab and the Camel is a popular fable amongst children across the world. It's about an Arab and his camel in the desert on a cold winter's night. The Arab is sleeping in his tent when the camel sticks his head inside and asks him if he can keep it in all night because he is cold. The Arab agrees. A while later, the camel inches further in, and asks if he can warm his neck. The Arab, who is a kind man, agrees. These allowances not being enough, the camel asks if he can put his legs inside the tent. This goes on through the night until the camel eventually asks the Arab if he can sleep inside the tent while the Arab sleeps outside it. We have one such camel in our house, but where the Arab wizened up to the camel's intentions and harnessed him to a tree outside, my parents, till date, haven't taken cognizance of the camel in our midst.

When the three brothers who owned this land sold it to my father—brothers who drank themselves to death after coming into money—they placed a man on it to keep vagrants off the land until the new owners started building on it. The man lived in a shack and rode a bicycle to the nearby village to buy his groceries.

When the plan for the houses was ready, my father decided to let the man stay and manage the labourers who would come to do the construction. Thus, the man became a foreman. When the buildings were completed, three years later, the foreman asked my father, who was a powerful politician by then, to make him the manager of the property.

As a child, I used to play in Rajiv Gandhi's lap. I once asked him why he let the barber cut his hair so short; clearly, I was too young to know about premature balding. He was kind to me, and affectionate—that is how I remember him. My father hero-worshipped the man. The two had been buddies since they were teenagers. They flew planes together and fought elections together, until Rajiv vanished and my father's hair turned white within the year. Rajiv Gandhi, of all the men I've seen my father associate with or surrounded by, is the only one I have fond memories of; the rest are pretty much like Suraj Singh, the camel.

Not only did Suraj Singh become the manager of the farm, but also a collector, messenger and delivery man. He became my parents' Man Friday, and to my brother and I, our nemesis. As we matured and came into our own, he spared no opportunity to discredit us to our parents. In a family already as fractious as ours, it was the last thing we needed.

While my father did his job, working towards the general good of his political constituency, Suraj Singh went about using his name to boost his net worth. When he had grown beyond the point his growth could be concealed, he told my parents he was doing exceptionally well with the farming he had started on his ancestral land. Clever camel!

Driving a German car to the farm every Sunday—the one day of the week our family has lunch together—Suraj Singh takes his seat at the head of the table. After 12 years of marriage, deciding I couldn't live with my in-laws any longer, I'd returned to the farm with my children over the summer holidays, to figure out how to break it to my husband that I needed autonomy and space back home in Mumbai. I was neither here nor there; I was in a limbo. I was the underdog so many women end up becoming when dealing with conflict in their marital homes. One fine Sunday, Suraj Singh came up with a solution for the problem that was me. He suggested to my parents that they pack me off to America. I'd be so busy, he said, cooking, cleaning, working and caring for the children out there, that I'd have little time and energy left to ponder over my lot in life. The pudge I'd piled on after giving birth to my boys, too, would shed off of me, all by itself. That he had the gall to make such a suggestion, even if it was half in jest, wasn't as surprising to me as the fact that my parents didn't flinch upon hearing it. The only person at the table who responded, and that, too, under his breath, was Suveer. "Why don't we send you, instead," he said. Live long, brother.

Suraj Singh, like Rasputin did to the Russian queen, has made himself indispensable to my mother. This Rasputin from the state of UP knows better than anyone whose back to rub, now that my father, the old tiger, is crippled. A fellow, to whom lying is an art, who, to a paper castle, is a pair of scissors, is inching closer and closer by the day, to becoming the brother my mother never had. Granted, this is an easy castle to shred, but that he did it, and profited from it, and is still doing it, speaks of the character of the camel I will hereafter refer to as Man Friday, or Rasputin.

Family intrigues aside, my chief concern, at the moment, is for my father's Alphonso mangoes. Feeling more like a drug lord on a drug run than a mother on a food run, donning a mask, goggles and a bandana, I was paying for my goods at the grocery store yesterday when I noticed a tempo offloading Alphonso mangoes in the parking lot. I went back today to buy a box for my father. A dozen mangoes were selling for 1,300 rupees. While buying them, I thought of the farmers who had grown them. Most of the Alphonso mangoes grown in India are exported. With no flights to take them abroad, the mango farmers will take a big hit. My only solace, thinking about their plight, was that I bought a box—and I had bought it for the greatest lover of mangoes who ever lived. I wanted to welcome my father home from the ICU with his favourite fruit.

My father wants to live. My father *has* to live—for me, for my brother, and for his grandchildren. I can't imagine a world without him. I can't imagine a world with the likes of Suraj Singh as lord and master.

Day 25

14 April 2020

I remember the actor Sanjay Dutt, at a dinner engagement in Mumbai, telling the guests at his table about his ordeal in isolation—my husband and I happened to be seated at that table. He had passed his time in a dank cell, lifting ants up to a hole high up in the wall—serving as a window—to help them reach freedom.

I may be going the Sanjay Dutt way. While I was doing yoga this morning, my nose to the ground, I saw a beetle lugging its dotted igloo over and across the blades of grass. A dragonfly flew past it while a tick trudged in the mud under it. The scene was whimsical, bringing to mind those mythical beings, gnomes, the midget guardians of underground treasures. The beetle's body looked like a gnome's red hat, balancing as it was, on a blade of grass. I had the sudden urge to dig and discover the creatures and objects hidden in the mud; springtails, earthworms, mud wasps and their paralysed food, spiders, an antique coin or an odd bone (no, not a bone—and if it has to be, let it be a dog's old bone and not a human femur!).

There aren't any magic mushrooms in this garden to transport me to the psychedelic peregrinations of my college days, and with no magnifying glass (I haven't been able to find the one I bought for the boys when they were small), and my poor eyesight, there'll be no investigations into the subterranean realms for me, today. I'll have to get my thrills from watching the winged creatures—those are aplenty; birds, butterflies, dragonflies and fireflies. My day is chalked out: one down, and it's anyone's guess how many more to go; cast, as we all are, under the shadow of a monster pandemic.

Day 26

15 April 2020

The Prime Minister has announced Lockdown 2.0. The second lockdown will last 20 days and comes with fresh guidelines. The first directive—which, I'm guessing, is required *only* in India—makes spitting in public places a punishable offense. Movement of goods and services, construction, e-commerce and agricultural activities are permitted under Lockdown 2.0. Pharmaceutical and fishing industries, too, will resume operations. However, malls, shops, movie halls, the railways and airline operators will remain shut.

Donald Trump has withdrawn US funding to the World Health Organisation, not a wise decision, in my opinion: there's a time to settle scores, and this is not it—not when experts are warning the world of an impending famine. The WHO needs all the support it can get right now.

50% of the staff in a ward in London has tested positive for the virus. There's a chronic shortage of protective gear, everywhere. Health workers in America are resorting to wearing garbage bags, while, in India, doctors are wearing raincoats and sunglasses for protection. Scientists have said that, to control the spread of the virus, intermittent lockdowns will be required till

2022. It will rise and fall in waves, never really going away until a vaccine is developed and administered to a large chunk of the global population. Based on a worldwide survey of patients, more women are contracting the disease than men (possibly because females constitute a large number of the frontline workers) but more men are dying from it. The reason for this could be the fact that women are biologically stronger. They have a more robust immune system. It's plausible, therefore, that our future leaders will not only be young but also female. The female-led nations of Norway, Finland, Iceland, Denmark, Taiwan, New Zealand and Germany have had the lowest infection and mortality rates so far. Considering that only 10% of heads of states are female, they've shown wiser leadership than their male counterparts during the pandemic.

The purples in the lawn have turned to ash. Flowers are drooping on their stalks. The wind is growing warmer. Roses have stopped making it to the vase in my room. Spring is turning to summer.

Day 27

16 April 2020

Thousands of migrant workers gathered at the Bandra Station on the last day of the first lockdown, hoping to board a train that would take them home. The police pushed the crowd into a huddle, like cattle in a pen, transforming it into a virus cluster in the making. The incident was followed by a political blame game over who spread the fake news that trains would be taking workers stranded in Mumbai back to their villages. The rumour got the workers' hopes up only to dash them, once again, thereby delivering a demoralising blow to the already jobless and hungry.

The frustration of being locked up is getting to everyone: Robin's been hitting his younger brother almost on a daily basis. He calls him "fat" and "pig". One of my sons is so thin that he has to be coerced into eating, while the other has to be stopped from overeating. In times of extraordinary uncertainty, eating is a comfort that many can't resist, and folks who feel like their lives are reeling out of control, gain power in starving. Violence and inwardness, eating and starving, laughing and crying: people's emotions are manifesting in extreme ways.

Life has become one big wtf!

Day 28

17 April 2020

My father has returned after four days in the hospital. Though he is weak in body, his spirit is strong. This was the first time he had stayed overnight at a hospital. I haven't been that lucky: I've had meningitis, mumps, hepatitis, malaria and typhoid; I've broken my ankle and dislocated my wrists while playing sports; I've given natural birth to two healthy babies (although one can't—or shouldn't—be called a patient when they're in hospital to give birth, I don't think). Many nights at the hospital I've spent. It's a bitch. I pray dad doesn't have to spend even one more. I'm happy to see him happy to be home, back to his castle. It gives me satisfaction to get the chance to sit beside him while he has his evening tea, to hold his hand, kiss his forehead and help him into his slippers. It brings meaning to my life.

Day 29

18 April 2020

Attacks on doctors continue in Ghaziabad, Indore and Mumbai. Why, in God's name, can't these people get it into their heads that if they catch this virus, and their symptoms worsen, they can die? They can carry it asymptomatically and kill their parents and grandparents with it. Are they not watching the news or listening to the radio?

Fear is the most powerful instigator. When I see terrified residents throwing stones at doctors visiting their slums to test them for the virus, and medics getting attacked by their own neighbours, memories of the Sikh riots during my childhood return to haunt me. Back then, fear was not the instigator, but retribution.

My father was in Russia when Indira Gandhi was assassinated. His Sikh friends—co-pilots and pilots who had flown with him when he used to work for the Indian Airlines—were waiting for him at the airport when he landed in the capital. They told him about the madness that was spreading on the streets—people were forming groups and setting innocent Sikhs on fire. The domino effect of violence had begun.

School was dismissed early that day, and I remember sitting in the bus behind two teachers. One was saying, "She's been shot several times." The other replied, "She could be dead." I didn't know who they were talking about but I sensed heaviness in the air—a heaviness tinged with fear.

The lady they were talking about was the same as the one I knew as Mrs G, the one who gifted me a toy cat on Christmas, the one whose house I enjoyed meals at with my family on happy occasions, the one who gave me my name before I was born.

The next day, it was eerily silent in our lane, which was usually noisy with children. As night descended, the silence became deafening. Piercing the dark silence, then, I heard a sound I hope to never hear again—the sound of a hundred male voices coming towards us all at once, as a single, resonant, angry yell. "Put out the lights," my mother screamed from the living room. The house went dark. I jumped into the trunk in the bedroom where we kept the sheets and blankets. That is as far as my memory goes.

What I know of what happened next comes from hearing the grown-ups talking the following day. The mob stopped in front of our gate. The neighbour's housekeeper, a brave Nepali man, came out and confronted the collective. He asked them what they wanted. Someone in the crowd said that our house had a Sikh driver; they'd come for him. The housekeeper told them that Jesse (Jaswinder) hadn't come to work that day. They threatened to burn our jeep parked outside the gate. The Nepali housekeeper convinced them, somehow, not to do it. The mob, then, turned to the house across the lane from us. A Sikh family was living in its garage. The father of the family was an electrician. The mob demanded that the electrician be brought out. The owner of the house emerged and confronted the mob. He was a Hindu. He told the mob that they would have to burn him and his house down before they could get to the Sikh family living on rent in his garage. He and the Nepali housekeeper from next door, the two of them blocked the mob's access to the garage by standing resolutely before the gate. There was much noise, and then the mob moved on.

I can never forget this story of courage from my lane in Panchsheel Park. And I can never forget how scared I was for my best friends, Gursimran Dhingra and Shallu Sodhi, both Sikh girls. Gursimran had a lovely house in Friends Colony; her parents were the nicest people I knew; she was the prefect of our class, an outstanding girl in every way: her house was burned to the ground.

My father can't forget those awful days, either; he's a Punjabi, after all. Several of his co-workers and friends lost their loved ones, and some perished. When I see visuals of people pelting stones at health workers, wounded doctors receiving treatment in hospitals, and sanitation workers getting lynched, I remember from the riots of my childhood what a lethal cocktail ignorance and illiteracy can make.

Ignorance is not bliss. Ignorance is ignorance. The only place it takes you is backwards—and that is not where we want to go.

Day 30

19 April 2020

Kali will dance her dance of destruction until she's done dancing.

10,000 people have died in New York. More people have lost their lives to the pandemic in America than in the recent wars fought by that country.

Modi's Lockdown 2.0 has brought with it greater woes for the Indian migrant worker. One took his own life today. Selling his last possession, his mobile phone, for 2,500 rupees, and leaving the amount to his wife and two children, he killed himself. Food urgently needs to be distributed to the people who don't have access to it. More community kitchens have to be set up in schools and temporary camps erected for migrant families to take refuge in. The poor form the majority of this country. They keep it going. And yet we don't value them like we should. When there's a national catastrophe, like an earthquake, drought or an epidemic, they are the first to go.

Amid rampant selfishness and ignorance, touching stories of good people helping others in need have emerged, like that of a policeman in a southern state who offered a lift to a couple walking along the road. The wife was in labour. He took them to a hospital and stayed on to make sure everything went alright. While giving birth, the mother needed blood. The policeman donated his blood to give her a new lease on life. From Delhi comes another story, of a family with three warriors; the father and son are practicing doctors and the daughter-in-law is a teacher at a government school, who is now teaching her students online. In their free time, the family distributes masks and bottles of hand sanitiser to the public. There is hope. Humanity is still alive. We will get through this. It is critical, though, that we remember such people—for these are the kinds of people we need to choose as leaders when the storm passes.

While the world's attention is diverted towards managing the deadly virus it had unleashed, China has gone ahead and arrested 14 pro-democracy activists in Hong Kong. Most notable of them is 81-year-old Martin Lee, known as the founding father of Hong Kong's democratic movement. Jimmy Lai, founder of the anti-establishment tabloid, *Apple Daily*, is the other big name.

We didn't collectively oppose China's brazen appropriation of the islands in the South China Sea; and so, they went ahead and built military installations on them. We're unable to hold them accountable for the pandemic—we're too busy saving our own lives. We mustn't stay silent about these influential activist-leaders getting arrested. The rogue nation, rogue and yet frighteningly systematic, has to be stopped. If we don't demonstrate strength in solidarity and stand up to it, China will call the shots after this crisis is over and we will *have* to obey. Switzerland has been exemplary in expressing solidarity with fellow nations in the pandemic. The Swiss have been displaying the flags of different countries on the Matterhorn Mountain and posting messages of love and empathy in support of nations combating the disease. They projected the Indian flag this week to give "hope and strength" to the Indians. It is precisely this kind of solidarity we need to stand up to China. We have but two choices; unite and fight, or prepare to be governed by a despotic regime.

Day 31

20 April 2020

I try to watch the television with detachment, but when I see patients gurgling in ventilators encasing their heads like space helmets, I feel it—what it must be like to be inside one of those things. You're looking through a glass shield over your face, shielding not you from others but others from you; oxygen pumped through a tube into your helmet for you to breathe. Breathing—the simple act of breathing—has become a luxury. We had taken so much for granted that we can't even take breathing for granted anymore.

The horridness of it all can be overwhelming. I feel the pain I'm witnessing because I have had pain, physical and emotional. The physical pain, intense as it was, didn't make the same lasting impression on me as the emotional pain; that remains inside me, lurking, perpetually, waiting for a chance to manifest. It's the cause of my temper that needs constant checking.

As a child, I would overhear my mother telling her friends that she had bruises in the shape of four-leaf clovers on her legs, where my hands had clenched her flesh to climb up onto her lap. I was a monster, she'd say. I began to believe it was true—that I was bad. But it all came into perspective when

I had children of my own: my formative self, the toddler, was trying to climb onto her mother's lap because she wanted to be held and cuddled. The problem was, my mother could express physical affection towards few people aside from my father. Like my mother-in-law, my mother had a history that made her this way. Just like I have a history that makes me the way I am.

My maternal grandfather was an ambassador from the International Monetary Fund to the United Nations, and a writer for *Time* and *Life* magazines. Contrary to my paternal grandfather, who renounced his responsibilities towards his progeny and became an ascetic, my maternal grandfather was in the habit of micro-managing his children's lives. When my mother was 13 years old, her parents relocated from Holland to Washington D.C. The couple had their third daughter after their move to the US. My mother was the eldest of the sisters, and most spirited—a combination of factors that made life rough for her in the household. Her father was a talented man but also a highly irritable one, especially when it came to noise. My mother was whacked on the head for the slightest sound she'd make when he was around, even if that sound was the turning of a page of a comic book. Back in those days, it was common for kids to get spanked every now and then, as many parents went by the old adage, "spare the rod and spoil the child". My grandfather was very conscious about looks and would call my mom skinny and flat-chested: she would have to swallow a spoonful of castor oil along with dinner to put on weight. Since my mother didn't get any pocket money, she worked as a salesgirl at a mall after school to buy herself the kind of clothes she liked. By the time she was 18, as a consequence of all these factors, she had come to believe that money and attention were the most important things in life. She also became very sensitive to touch.

On graduating from high school, my mother bought herself an airline ticket to Taiwan. She wanted to study Chinese art, get as far away from her father, and live on her own terms. But, as the old saying goes, "man proposes and God disposes". Destiny intervened. She met my father on the flight, and didn't get further than New Delhi. The couple eloped. And the rest is history—a history where I come in. My father was a pilot and went to work for three days at a time. When he returned from his flights, I would run into his arms, unable to contain my excitement. This irritated my mother. She would instruct my grandmother, who I called *Badi Ma*, to take me away to the other room. I have never been a competitive person; I've always seen myself as my own chief competitor. I couldn't keep up with the endless competition for my father's attention.

The pain of being sent away, repeatedly, remained. It made me a lamb. I was a lamb simmering in thick broth, bogged down, low, nowhere to go. But then, one glorious day, the lamb decided to become a tiger. So, now, though I like to be fussed over and listened to, like most people do, I no longer *need* to be—that is what choosing to be a tiger over a lamb does. Once you're a tiger, you may *want* attention and validation, but you don't *need* it. All you really need is *roti, kapda aur makaan* (food, clothing and a roof over your head). When you no longer need adoration or validation from others, you develop an understanding of yourself; and this, inevitably, leads to self-love. And what self-love does, apart from giving you strength, is it makes you more attractive to other people. You attract love, without trying. That we are the products of our histories—sometimes victims of it—

doesn't mean that we don't have a choice. We can choose not to allow the negative experiences of the past to cloud our future. We need only to view the past as a teacher and learn the lessons it is trying to teach us. The rewards of this higher level of learning are sweet—wisdom, maturity, and fulfilment in life.

Day 32

21 April 2020

"Doctors must be killed," rang the outraged voices in the mob. I watched CCTV footage on the news, of around a hundred people pushing past a police barricade, carrying rods and knives, throwing stones and breaking streetlights. The incident which took place in Karnataka was planned and provoked, according to some reports, by the Tablighi Jamaat. The miscreants that organised the assemblage were clearly ignorant of the fact that this sort of behaviour achieves little more than to fuel the negative sentiment prevalent in members of the majority towards the minority groups.

Maharashtra has reported 552 cases in a single day. Of the 12 new deaths in the state, six were in Mumbai. I try not to worry too much about my loved ones there. Spending time in the garden helps. Despite my efforts, I haven't found the magnifying glass; it's possible the boys took it to Mumbai after one of their visits to the farm. I've been sitting in the *Hawa Mahal*, surrounded by thick grasses stubbornly guarding the secret lives of the multitudinous insects sheltering therein, reading a book called *H is for Hawk*, by a woman named Helen Macdonald. The book is a memoir about the time the writer unexpectedly lost her father to a heart attack. She had always wanted to be a falconer, from childhood, but after the death of her father, the idea became an obsession. She bought herself a Goshawk and started training it. The memoir is about the difficult task of training this wildest of beasts and, through her intense love for it, healing from the deep grief she was feeling from the loss of her father. I looked up from my book for a moment and saw the black kite, who I've named Baaz, fly past, low enough for me to see its head searching for prey and the feathers on its wings. Gliding against a deep-blue sky full of fluffy white clouds, like the clouds seen from an airplane cruising at 20,000 feet above land, the sight of the raptor uplifted my soul.

After spending so many days in lockdown, people are longing to go for a walk beside a river or through a forest, or to simply sit under a tree in a park. They've formed groups on social media where they share images of rocks or strips of bark and flowers taken from outside their homes. As billions of us are imprisoned behind concrete walls, we're realising the value of nature in our lives like never before. Research suggests that spending time in natural surroundings has a calming effect on human beings—our longing to be in nature in this stressful and uncertain juncture is proof.

The youth were demanding restrictions on the use of plastics that end up polluting rivers and oceans, carbon emission reductions to curtail global warming, and stricter laws on poaching animals and clearing forests. We blindsighted them. America pulled out of the Paris Agreement. None of the countries that signed the Agreement reduced their carbon emissions to the prescribed levels. What do they have in mind, the top brass? There's never going to be an Earth II, no matter how hard they try to make the moon and Mars home planets. I don't want to live inside a biosphere on an inhospitable rock, no matter how pretty and hospitable they try to make it: a cage is a cage. Why not fight for the earth! Only wimps surrender to their circumstances. Only losers give up. All we have to do is curb our greed, and use only what we need. Come on, is that so hard to do!

Day 33

22 April 2020

The Prime Minister has introduced a new law, declaring any violent attack on the health professionals as a non-bailable offense, punishable by a seven-year jail term. Finally, a remedy for the madness!

A meme is doing the rounds on social media, claiming that Nostradamus, the 16th-century oracle, predicted the pandemic. In his book, *Les Prophéties*, the seer made predictions in cryptic quatrains. The most famous of these are the death of Henry II, the French Revolution and the bombing of Hiroshima and Nagasaki. He penned the exact year of the Great Fire of London. Referring to air travel, he prophesied, "People will travel safely through the sky." He described World War I and the flu epidemic that killed over 50 million people after it. He predicted the rise of Hitler, who he called Hisler.

The viral meme is as follows:

There will be a twin year (2020)
from which will rise a queen (corona)
who will come from the east (China)

and who will spread a plague (virus)
in the darkness of night, on a country
with 7 hills (Italy) and will transform
the twilight of men into dust (death),
to destroy and ruin the world.
It will be the end of the world economy as you know it.

A writer and occult enthusiast, Rae Alexander, wrote on 6 April on KQED, that he believes the quatrain in the viral meme is not the one predicting the pandemic. According to him, it is the following quatrain that makes the prediction:

> In the feeble lists, great calamity
> through America and Lombardy.
> The fire in the ship, plague and captivity;
> Mercury in Sagittarius, Saturn waning.

Nostradamus refers to the sick and the dead as "the feeble lists", writes Alexander, while the words "plague and captivity" are self-explanatory. Lombardy is a region in northern Italy. America and Italy have been the worst hit by the virus. In December 2019, Mercury entered Sagittarius—that's when the world became aware of the first cases of the disease. On 21 March, Saturn moved into Aquarius—that's when New York went into lockdown. The ship Nostradamus is referring to in this quatrain, according to Alexander, is the *Grand Princess*, which docked in Oakland on 9 March, with 21 confirmed cases of the virus on board. It could be any ship, however, since multiple ships became stranded at sea for having cases on board.

I was mystified by the occult in my youth and read extensively on it, including a translation of *Les Prophéties*, from where the meme was inspired. I can understand why the prophecy alluding to "the queen" is tickling people's imaginations. When humans are confronted by uncertainty, they tend to get anxious: it's the nature of the beast. The more anxious the people get, the more active their imaginations get. And when anxiety and ignorance mix, they can have devastating consequences; the Sikh riots of 1984 and the recent attacks on health workers are cases in point. Moreover, anxiety is contagious; it can form a cluster and spread from person to person. It can make people senseless, and sometimes, ridiculous.

The real-life tale of the three Jat brothers, who sold this land to my father, is known to our staff. They know that one of them died in an accident while driving drunk, another died in a 5-star hotel room, and the third, well, no one knows exactly how the third brother died and if his body was ever found. All they knew is that alcohol did them in. On cold winter nights, the members of the staff would make a fire outside their quarters and sit around it, talking in hushed tones about the ill-fated brothers. The tale filled their eyes with wonder and spooked them to the marrow in their bones.

One summer night, the wonder spilled from the electrician's eyes into his imagination. Finding it too hot to sleep with his family in their room, he decided to spend the night outside on the *charpai*. In the middle of the night, he felt the ropes of the charpai tighten and weigh down. He opened his eyes and, in the dim orange of the courtyard lamp, saw a tall man wearing a turban sitting beside him on the *charpai*. In the heat of the night, he shivered. The turbaned man asked him for a match. But Rajesh, the electrician, noticed that the man didn't have a cigarette in his hand. As the spectre stared at him with distant, disturbing eyes, Rajesh covered his head with his sheet and remained that way till morning came.

After Rajesh related the incident to the other staff members, more sightings were reported of the turbaned Jat. Someone saw his silhouette in the darkness under the water tank, smoke from his cigarette snaking its way up and disappearing into the light. He was heard knocking on someone else's door, *rasp rasp rasp*, a pause, then, *rasp rasp rasp*, through the night. He was seen wandering alone in the lawn, his shadow trailing behind him. A child saw him in a fog.

The stories, at long last, reached my father. Calling the lot of them, he said, "Don't be so damned superstitious!" Coincidence or common sense—I'll never know which it was—but the sightings of the turbaned Jat ceased.

Day 34

23 April 2020

Researchers at the Oxford Vaccine Group and the Jenner Institute have identified a potential vaccine candidate for the virus. The vaccine, called Chadox1, is gaining recognition as the most suitable vaccine technology. The researchers have said that the first batch of 1 million doses will be ready to be administered by September. While the world is holding its breath, hunkered down at home, and in some cases, in bunkers, waiting for a vaccine, wildlife continues to reclaim territory. A coyote was seen near the Golden Gate Bridge—an animal not seen in San Francisco for decades. A pack of wild boars has made a small town in Israel home. Crocodiles were seen sunbathing on a beach in Mexico. A cougar was roaming the streets of the Chilean capital. Dolphins have returned to the Ganges in Uttar Pradesh, India.

Day 35

24 April 2020

In this particular scene of the science fiction film we're all actors in, I'm driving along an empty road with not a soul in sight, but for police personnel in masks standing at intersections. An occasional car goes past me; sometimes it's a crumpled can on four wheels belonging to a villager and sometimes a Mercedes-Benz. There's no difference between the dented car and the shiny one. In this diseased world, the Mercedes has lost its place as a status symbol. Its driver, the rich man, has become like everyone else, and is doing what everyone else is doing—looking for food.

The poor man in his rubber slippers is in line ahead of the rich man in his Max Air Adidas shoes. Standing 2 m apart, maintaining social distance, they're waiting to buy vegetables at the only store they're allowed to buy them at in a 5 km radius. The rich man buys more food while the poor man buys less—that's the only difference between them. In this fiction film, we've all been beaten into sameness; and I'd argue it's not a bad thing. The rich needed to be reminded that they are just as human as the poor waiting in line behind them. Today, the poor man was ahead of the rich man, by virtue of arriving earlier.

The world ruled by the virus is a first-come-first-serve world, in every way. If the virus decides to come for the rich man, neither his shoes nor his car and nor his bank balance can save him. We've all become equal in the truest sense, for the first time, and only because this horrible episode in our modern history has forced us to it: horrible for us humans, but for the earth, a long overdue time to breathe.

Day 36

25 April 2020

There is hope in the air, much-needed hope at a time the virus has put 1.5 billion children out of school in 125 countries: UK has conducted the first human trials for a vaccine. I'm cautiously optimistic, for the news has come alongside another, more sinister, report. An asymptomatic positive man, who dined at a restaurant in China, infected nine other diners at the eatery; what makes this shudder-worthy is that the tables were set wide apart and everyone at the restaurant was practicing social distancing. Scientists are exploring the possibility that the air conditioning caused the virus to spread. People are worried that, if breathing recycled air can spread the virus, life won't return to normal until everyone on the planet is vaccinated.

Blackie killed a monkey. While its group gathered around its limp body, the children made a ring around the group and gawked at the bloody wound in the fallen animal's stomach. Blackie is small and thin but in no way does she lack courage. The macaques have rapidly multiplied and formed groups that fight noisy battles that often end in violence. One actually jumped onto my shoulders from the wall. When I waved my arms about, screaming, it jumped off again. The children are afraid to walk around the farm by themselves. A macaque bit Blackie so viciously on her head, about two weeks ago, that her skull bone was showing. Instead of sobering her down, the incident made the dog more aggressive towards the monkeys. The children see what she did as a revenge killing. The sad drama ended only when the gardener took the dead monkey and buried it beside the pond.

The weather is getting hotter and drier. The frog outside my room has gone quiet. But I did hear Lakshmi, our friendly neighbourhood elephant. She is well. That made me happy.

Day 37

26 April 2020

Thunder punctuated the night, and in the morning, came the rain. I dreamt that I was in a hotel room with my husband and a friend. The television in the room was bristling with static, the bedside tables were covered with empty wrappers and the air was stale; we'd been there for days. Water seeping through the compromised window casing dripped from the curtains and onto the music system on the carpet. I venture out of the room, as if for the first time, to find a housekeeper. I come across one pushing a cart in the corridor. I inform her about the dripping that was happening on the electronics. "You may want to look into that," I say. I notice some packets of imported cookies on her cart. I bundle the packets into my arms like an infant. *I've got to take these,* I think. *We won't be getting imported cookies for a long time—not until the borders open.*

My dream could have something to do with the fact that, after 36 days of living apart, my husband and I are having less and less to talk about. He tells me about the cook who can't cook, our three cats and the dog, and Netflix—a lot about Netflix. I tell him about the children, about how they fight, about how they demand for things I can't give them, about how they don't stick to the timings set for meals and sleep—about how they don't do a damn thing without my having to exert enormous energy into getting them to do it. If I'm not firm with the boys, they won't have a bath or do their homework or stop playing video games. When I share my frustration with my husband, he says, "It's okay, they'll mature." That doesn't help: it doesn't make them behave any better. It doesn't make me *feel* any better. It sounds distant. So distant. My whole world has become about caring for these two children. I feel alone. I've been alone. This journal is a lifesaver. It's my friend, my confidante, my alter ego, my partner and mirror. It's the surface off of which I bounce my ideations.

Walking around the farm after the rain, I enjoy the touch of the wind on my face and its wordless whispering in my ears. I watch the purple flowers blanketing a tree in the *Hawa Mahal*, that had turned ashen by the heat, lifting off like helicopters and spinning through the air to land on the grass. Some of them still hold on to their flecks of purple. Like their friends fallen before them, they, too, will soon lose their colour and fade into the mud.

The wind whips up into a small storm, and the ashen flowers, like birds sharing one mind, rise off the tree and fly away in a flock. I go to the pond, where giant leaves fallen from the Banyan sail on the choppy surface of the water, transporting insects to the islands of reeds, where the geese lay eggs that never hatch. Wind. Wind. Wind brushing against me, going inside and out of me as I breathe. Returning to the *Hawa Mahal*, my kurta balloons like an umbrella. The wind chimes have become temple bells, sounding an alarm: the thunder god has awoken. He has started his rumbling. It's like the rumbling of the rocket blasting off from earth, tearing through the sky, taking the three astronauts into the deep and open space. They are up there now, watching the lights of New York, out, and of Paris and Rome, and the unseasonal rain over the Indo-Gangetic Plain. Eating their space food from packets, they view these events with detachment. They look at each day as a blessing: the earth is still there, the rivers are still flowing into the seas, the clouds are still moving over their homes; it's all there. I, too, see each day as a blessing, even the days that are harder than others. I'm trying to see the world like the black kite, Baaz; I'm trying to observe what's happening around me, and *to* me, from a vantage point above myself. I accept that nothing is in my control, right now, and so I pay less attention to my circumstances and more to the larger picture. There is something to be learned from the larger picture.

Day 38

27 April 2020

In Noida and Surajkund, children run after food vans on hungry stomachs. The vans are surrounded by hundreds of families as soon as they arrive, but not even half the people have eaten, when the food runs out. The rest will have to wait till the next day, when the vans, hopefully, return. Migrant workers are bearing the brunt of the lockdown; they've reached the end of their savings, and for many, their threshold for pain.

An announcement declaring which states will lift the lockdown and which will continue with it is expected on the 3rd of May. Many people are of the opinion that work *has* to begin. I have no opinion. All I know for certain is that the virus is highly contagious: it spreads when an individual inhales the respiratory droplets released into the air when an infected person talks, coughs or sneezes; it can remain suspended in the air for up to three hours; it can survive on clothes and surfaces for days; it can be contracted by a person when he or she touches a contaminated object and then touches their nose, eyes or mouth. The infection starts in the throat and goes into the lungs. For people 65 years and older, or with serious underlying medical conditions, it can be fatal, causing severe respiratory illnesses like pneumonia. It's a sneaky bug; an individual can be walking around with it, asymptomatic, and yet spread it to hundreds of people without ever knowing it. It has mutated into ten different strains that are spreading in different parts of the country and around the world. That is why I have no opinion in regards to repeated lockdowns. People are starving because of them, but many lives have also been saved due to them. Presently, the central government is considering a staggered lifting of the second lockdown for districts with low numbers of cases.

A sickle moon is hanging above the Banyan beside the pond. Ramzan has begun. Followers of the Muslim faith are upset they're not allowed to congregate during the holy month, and even on Eid. There is one man who has stood out as an inspiration to the aggrieved: I watched his story on the news. The man had toiled his whole life to make enough money to go on Hajj, but now, due to the pandemic, he has forsaken his life-long dream and is spending his savings on feeding the hungry. This is the most righteous story to have emerged in this holy month, not only for followers of the Muslim faith but of all religions.

Day 39

28 April 2020

Wearing a nurse's uniform, the mayor of Mumbai visited hospitals and personally attended to patients; her unique gesture gave a much-appreciated boost to the morale of the overworked frontline workers combating the virus.

Lost, dry, looking for wetness, a frog that had strayed into the house plunged into my toilet bowl (frogs and other critters tend to slip into the house after heavy rains at the farm, thanks to the servants leaving the doors open behind them). As a teenager, I used to reach into the bowl and rescue lost and frightened critters (some were big old toads!); and sometimes, mice. When I tell my sons about it, they say, "Gross mom, how could you do that?" I've never been squeamish about creepy crawlies; I've seen cobras and garden snakes here, and monitor lizards as long as my leg and strong as a boar.

The rain shower got the monkeys into a romantic mood; I saw a couple copulating on the roof of the cabin where my children do their online schooling. One peed on me while I was exercising under my favourite Peepul, the one beside the swimming pool. The servants have kept pet rabbits in a cage at the back of the farm. Whitey poked her nose through the wire mesh and pulled one out and killed it. I want a baby bunny, but when I go back to Mumbai, I won't be able to take it with me. I don't want to adopt a bunny and cuddle it, and make it feel special, only to return it to a cage outside in the elements, with all the other rabbits. Animal shelters are emptying out as people are adopting animals to help them deal with their loneliness or boredom during the lockdowns. I just hope they don't neglect or return the pets to the shelters when life goes back to normalcy—whatever that will be after the scourge is done with its ravenous trek around the globe. Today, I got Robin to fix the cage with a shoestring, so that Whitey can't get to the rabbits. I achieved a milestone, regarding Whitey, that warrants a mention—I've managed to train her to sit and stay (though, sadly, I can't stop her from killing).

It's Sunday. I've made bread pudding for dessert. Relationships in the family are marginally better since Man Friday stopped coming to the farm as often as he used to—only a disease on a global scale could stop this raspy Rasputin from visiting the queen.

Day 40

29 April 2020

I was honoured when my father extended his foot and asked me to cut his toenails. As I got to work, we started chatting about our holiday in Egypt. My parents were under pressure during my last two years at university: the Congress government was out of power and numerous cases had been slapped on my father by the Opposition. Whenever I asked my mother for a ticket to return home on vacation, she'd say, "It isn't a good time for us," and that "You should stay on in America." To see no one from my family for that long, and at such a tender age, was rough. I attended courses and did an internship at a local television station during the breaks between semesters. Upon my graduation, my parents agreed to take me on a holiday to Egypt; it was a long-standing desire of mine to visit the Nile Delta and see the archaeological treasures of its ancient and enigmatic civilisation. I reminded my father about how we sailed the Nile on a Nubian boat, and saw the 5,000-year-old mummy of a nobleman we had the special privilege of viewing, in a cavern at Saqqara. All of the man's parts were perfectly intact—and I mean *all*. It was clear he was robust and handsome in life. "Oh, so you were with us in Egypt?" my father suddenly said. I glanced at him in disbelief. *How could he not remember my being there?* I thought. And just as my attention got diverted from the task at hand, for that instant, I nicked the loose skin on the side of my father's fingernail. "Ahhh," he groaned. I was mortified. I had cut my children's nails since they were babies, but I had literally never nicked them; how could I have made such a mistake? The cut was so tiny that I couldn't see it but the drop of blood that oozed from it scared me as much as it scared my father. I applied pressure on the cut and had a servant get Neosporin powder and a Band-Aid from my room. I put them on his finger, and then he asked me to leave.

Lying on my bed, feeling guilty and angry at myself, I wept. I had lost my concentration and nicked my father, a recovering heart patient. I got up and put on my gym shoes and went to the treadmill in the changing-room by the pool. I kept running until I dripped sweat like blood and couldn't breathe.

At night, I had two Patiala pegs from an old bottle of scotch I found lying around the house and crawled into bed. In the thick of sleep, I heard my son, Rishi, crying. I got up to find him in the kitchen, begging for breakfast from the cook. He was telling Rishi that it wasn't time yet, he'd come too early.

"Make it yourself," he said. When it comes to my brother's children, the cook is the goddamn Energiser Bunny, running to their room with trays laden with food and calling on the intercom throughout the day to ask if they needed or wanted anything. It wasn't that I had become a second-grade citizen in what was once my home that was bothering me—I was used to that—or that I'd accidentally nicked my father's finger; what was really bothering me was that my father was losing his memory. His mind was becoming selective of memories; and the ones of me didn't appear to be important enough to hold on to. He was joining millions of elderly people caught in a world of forgetting and fading. With the passing of each day, I witness his slow transformation into a child. It's hard to accept. But I must accept it, and I must forgive: I have to forgive him for forgetting me. I have to forgive him for forsaking me, for, as he diminishes, so diminish my say and my rights. Unfortunately for me, I've never been good at playing the game. There are master players here. I watch from the sidelines—and write.

I baked a cherry pie this afternoon. Tomorrow, I will bake cinnamon cookies. The day after tomorrow, I'll bake a chocolate cake for the children, and for this, here, my family.

Day 41

30 April 2020

At last, I can sleep peacefully: my father's finger has healed. The stents inserted in his arteries are showing results; he is regaining his strength. Rishi accompanied me to his room today to entertain him with stories about school. But dad was in the mood of telling his own tales. I knew most of them but he was so lucid this morning that he included names and details I hadn't heard before. The story of my father's life is the stuff movies are made of—a one of a kind.

My father, Capt. Satish Kumar Sharma, was born in 1947 in Secunderabad, to Punjabi Brahmin parents. His maternal grandfather was Amar Chand Sharma, a self-made man who started a construction company near Hyderabad in 1914. The company built dams and laid railway tracks for the British government. It employed thousands of labourers and work animals, and owned heavy machinery like road rollers, excavators, forklifts, jeeps and trucks. Satish's grandfather would take him to the site of the Khasapur Dam, the project the company was working on when he was a child. As a 10-year-old, Satish got to sit in the cockpit of a truck, his feet barely touching the pedals, and take it for a spin. He was driven every weekend in his grandfather's car, the first of its kind in the state, to the house of an Anglo-Indian couple to spend the day and learn proper English. When he went to school, Satish's grandmother would pack vegetarian snacks like *aloo* or *gobhi parantha* in his tiffin box. His best friend, a Muslim boy named Ismail, asked him, one day, if he could try his *parantha*. The friends exchanged tiffin boxes; and that's how the Brahmin boy tasted meat for the first time, mutton biryani, and became a lifelong lover of non-vegetarian cuisine.

When Satish entered puberty, tough times befell the family as his father decided to become an ascetic and move with his wife and three children to New Delhi. The boy lost the comforts and security of his life in Hyderabad, overnight. Satish's mother was an intelligent woman—she spoke five languages—but she was not well-educated according to conventional standards, English being a language she learned much later, when her Dutch daughter-in-law came into the picture. Satish had to find a way to go to school. Upon making friends in the poor neighbourhood, where the family landed up, he discovered that The Mother's International School was one of the finest in the city. It also happened to be close enough to commute on bicycle.

Satish got onto his bicycle and rode to The Mother's International School. He walked into the principal's office and requested to be admitted to the school. After a short interview, the principal asked the boy where he had learned to speak such good English. Satish told her about his visits to the Anglo-Indian household back in Hyderabad. Impressed by his eloquence and confidence, the principal granted him admission into the school.

An air force pilot would often visit the school campus. The students joked about his crush on the principal, Indu. Presumably, she fancied him, too, for he started teaching a course at the school. "Anyone who joins my aeronautics course will get a free ride in a glider," he told Satish's class when he came to recruit students for the course. Satish was first to raise his hand.

In his final year at school, Satish became the student council president. Jawaharlal Nehru was raising funds for the war effort against China at the time. Satish collected donations and, along with the principal, went to the Prime Minister's house and handed him a cheque on behalf of the students. This was his first meeting with a member of the Gandhi family.

Rajiv, the Prime Minister's grandson, would come in his grandfather's chauffeur-driven car to the Delhi Gliding Club, where Satish, too, came to learn gliding. Rajiv stopped, one day, and gave Satish a lift, putting his bicycle in the boot of the car. The two became friends.

Later, Rajiv left for London to pursue his further education and Satish returned to Hyderabad to attend the Hyderabad Flying Club. Jawaharlal Nehru died and Indira Gandhi became Prime Minister.

Satish's younger brother got to know that Rajiv was accompanying his mother on an official visit to Hyderabad. Satish looked up the phone number to the Governor's residence and asked to speak to Rajiv. The Prime Minister's son came on the line. "What are you doing in Hyderabad?" he asked, surprised. Satish told him that he was staying at his grandfather's house and attending flight school. Satish was then 17, and Rajiv, 19. Both were training to become pilots. Rajiv told Satish to come over to the Governor's residence. By then, Satish's grandfather, too, had died. He took his grandfather's old car to the Governor's residence and brought his friend home for lunch with the family.

When he was 21, Satish returned to Delhi, and became the youngest pilot to join the Indian Airlines. Satish and Rajiv flew together for the carrier, Satish as pilot and Rajiv as co-pilot. They married and had children.

A polo player, who was a close friend of Maneka and Sanjay Gandhi, lived in the corner house on the same lane as Satish. Having returned after a three-day flight schedule, Satish was asleep in the early afternoon, when the polo player came home to see him. Satish was alarmed by the visit, since the man had never dropped by before; he was part of Sanjay's group of friends while Satish belonged to Rajiv's group. Satish got out of bed and invited him in. The polo player informed him that Sanjay Gandhi was dead.

Satish made a call to Rajiv, who was in Italy, on holiday with his wife. Rajiv told Satish that he was afraid that something like this would happen: his brother was a daredevil and wouldn't listen to anyone who advised him to be careful. Devastated by the death of her younger son, Mrs Gandhi turned to her elder son for comfort and assistance. Rajiv left his job as a pilot and joined his mother in politics.

When Rajiv was in the thick of it, he asked Satish to quit his job at the airline and assist him. "You're the only man I can trust," he said. Satish joined his friend in the fray.

Indira Gandhi was assassinated and Rajiv became the Prime Minister. Then, one fateful day, Rajiv, too, was assassinated. His decision to send the Indian Peace-Keeping Force (IPKF) to Sri Lanka, to keep the peace between the Liberation Tigers of Tamil Eelam (LTTE) and the Sri Lankan troops, turned out to be fatal for him. The LTTE was created as a result of the antagonism between the Singhalese majority and the Tamil minority in the island nation. The rebel group had killed 13 soldiers in 1983, causing the war to officially begin between the Sri Lankan government and the LTTE. The mission of the Indian soldiers was to help keep the peace, but it soon became to disarm the LTTE. When the IPKF was pulled out in the summer of 1990, the warring resumed. In an interview to *Sunday* magazine (21–28 August 1990), during his election campaign, Rajiv Gandhi said that if he came back to power, he would send the IPKF back to Sri Lanka to dismantle the LTTE. Prabhakaran, the head of the rebel group, used this statement to stir resentment towards Rajiv in the Tamil population. He accused Rajiv of siding with the Sri Lankan government against the Tamil people of Sri Lanka. The resentment this instigated in the Tamils, even in India, towards Rajiv Gandhi, enabled Prabhakaran to get the support he needed to plot Rajiv's assassination. It was a revenge killing. Rajiv had meant well. He was young. He was raw. He didn't always take the best advice. The combination of these factors led to his untimely demise.

During a visit to America, on a free ticket from the Indian Airlines, when he was 23, Satish saw veterans of the Vietnam War—many of whom were younger than himself—returning from the battlefield, irrevocably broken in body and spirit. It was a proxy war, fought between western democracy and Russian and Chinese communism: the giants were flexing their muscles in the tiny nation of Vietnam. It was then that Satish formed the opinion that interfering in the internal affairs of other nations was best avoided; using diplomatic means was the safest and most humane way of resolving conflicts. The decision to involve boots on the ground, he came to believe, should only be taken if there's an imminent threat to the sovereignty of one's own nation.

Rajiv's death came as a terrible blow to Satish. He never recovered from the loss of his best friend.

Rajiv's widow, Sonia, took control of the Congress party. Satish would go and meet her every afternoon, just like he did with Rajiv. There was a tussle in the party for the Prime Minister's post. Arjun Singh and Sharad Pawar were the frontrunners. Satish advised Sonia to consider another name— Narasimha Rao. He had been the Chief Minister of Andhra Pradesh and had served in the cabinets of both Indira and Rajiv Gandhi. He was a scholar and a linguist. He had a clean image.

Narasimha Rao became the next Prime Minister. Capt. Satish Sharma became the Minister for Petroleum and Natural Gas in his cabinet.

This is the story my father told his grandson about his life.

Day 42

1 May 2020

Robin catches fireflies in the garden before bedtime and releases them in his bedroom. He falls asleep watching the tiny luminous beings, fluttering around him, giving him an exclusive last performance.

Later in the night, I stroll through the mulberry grove, where a township of fireflies flits in the underwood. I'm transported, once again, to the mythical world of the gnomes. Real creatures appear imagistic and the unreal begins to feel real. In the absence of artificial sounds of airplanes roaring through the sky, and rubber wheels and horns out on the street, I watch the infinitesimal live fires twinkling in glorious silence. There is truth in what the seers say: existence *is* bliss.

Day 43

2 May 2020

The waning of my father's newer memories and the waxing of his old ones could be contagious, I'm afraid, like the virus; I seem to be experiencing something similar, lately. The one year in my life when everything came together to form a perfect shit storm has returned in striking detail to the forefront of my mind—the year 1996.

It was the year of my parent's 25th marriage anniversary. My mother had planned to celebrate it by renewing their wedding vows in a grand ceremony. My father, however, wasn't as keen as her to go through with the plan because he was under intense scrutiny: a raid on the farm was imminent. Relatives poured in from far and wide and I returned to Delhi from college in America, just for three days, to attend the events.

Seated cross-legged before the sacrificial fire, wiping the sweat off his face with a crisp white handkerchief, white as his kurta-pyjama, my father looked tense. At the cocktail party later that evening, I was keeping members of the family from Hyderabad amused, trying to diffuse the tension that had spread from my father's creased forehead to his relatives, when Suraj Singh informed me in a whisper that a journalist and a cameraman had jumped over the boundary wall and were headed to the venue. He was quite drunk, I could see, so I decided to investigate the matter personally.

In the dimly lit driveway, half way between the gate and the lawn where the party was under way, I came across a petite woman. The cameraman who was with her had jumped back over the wall, leaving her to fend for herself. Sounding like the American-educated student of Mass Media that I was, I told the journalist that she was trespassing on private property. She replied, "The people have a right to know what's going on here." I told her that this was yellow journalism. "Who has attended this party—the people have a right to know," she persisted, getting louder. When I offered to escort her to the gate, she vehemently argued with me, and refused to go. Before I could consider what to do next, Suraj Singh whipped out a pistol and pointed it at her. I had no idea he had started carrying a weapon. I know the power a firearm can give you when it comes into your hand: I used to be a regular at the shooting range near Purana Qila on my vacations. I humbly profess that I was so skilled with the 12-bore shotgun that my coach told me that, if I hadn't been an American citizen, I could have been on the Indian national team. As much as I enjoyed shooting, I never wanted to own a gun. For me, it was a recreational sport, like any other. But that didn't make me oblivious to the ego boost holding a firearm in your hands can give you. And when it comes in the hands of people like Suraj Singh, it brings out the monster within, the Ravana, godfather of Rasputin. Such an individual feels invincible, just with that one, single, metallic object strapped to his ass. I brought Singh's hand down to his side, afraid he would accidently pull the trigger, and instructed him to return to the party. "This is not where you want to be, woman, not with this fellow around," I told the journalist, who was visibly shaken after having had a gun pointed at her. "Please, let me show you the way out."

Back at the party, ordering a drink to calm my nerves, I pondered how many people Suraj Singh had pointed that pistol at, and whether I should tell my father about what had just happened; the man was perturbed, I didn't want to aggravate his situation. Suraj Singh had allegedly molested a 16-year-old *pahari* girl who used to work at the farm. My grandmother enjoyed watching the doll-faced youngster from her wheelchair, sitting beside her, sewing floral garlands to drape on the idols in the family shrine. One day, the maid left on holiday and never returned. When my grandmother called to ask her why, she told her that she would never come back because Suraj Singh fondled her every chance he got. My parents didn't believe it, or refused to believe it. I imagined Singh waiving his revolver at her, too, and, then, all of a sudden—perhaps it was my intuition, or just plain old suspicion—I envisioned him setting it on the table in a negotiation and glibly watching the other person recoil. Just the other week, he showed it to my sons, much to my chagrin. He has a license for the firearm, and so there's really nothing I can do about it. Besides, the situation has come to such a point that, either way, license or not, I can say or do nothing about this Rasputin. I may be thrown off the farm. He never will.

On my way back to college, I was stopped at the Los Angeles Airport, singled out by the airport authorities. I was made to strip, buck naked, and bend over under the watchful gaze of a pair of gargantuan black policewomen. With a six-hour layover in Amsterdam, I had already had an exhausting journey. The delay due to the search caused me to miss my connecting flight to San Diego, my college town; I would now have to wait another four hours to catch the next one. Fighting tears, I told myself to look at the bright side—at least I wasn't subjected to a cavity search.

While I was undergoing my ordeal at the LAX, 120 policemen descended upon the farm in New Delhi. It was still full of relatives from Hyderabad. My grandmother sent a relative to every room and into every bathroom, to keep a close watch on the policemen as they raided the premises; we had been warned that the cops could plant incriminating material during the raid. The men searched for six hours. Nothing was found. Even so, 40 journalists landed up at the gate the next day. Our four Great Danes came in handy; along with the two Gorkha guards posted at the entrance, they kept the reporters at bay. (The petite journalist was lucky that the Danes were tied up on the night of the anniversary!) The Sunday edition of a leading newspaper featured a cartoon, that weekend, showing Capt. Satish Sharma sunbathing on a diving board over a swimming pool, wearing sunglasses and sipping on a cocktail, while at his front gate, two Gorkha guards astride a giant dog were keeping a pack of reporters out.

People thought we had Italian tiles. They thought we had sacks of cash. They thought many things I wasn't even aware of. Our pool was tiled with Indian tiles. Indeed, the farm is built as per local land laws. A little scandal doesn't hurt, some say. But that only applies to rock stars, and *not* to politicians and their families. The strip search I was subjected to, I am convinced, happened because the Indian authorities suspected I had returned to Delhi to take valuables back to the US to hide for my parents, like, who knows, gold biscuits or bricks. I had no gold bricks in my bag or biscuits in my vagina. On the contrary, I was kept on such a tight budget by my mother that I was as poor as your regular American college student.

Prior to 1996, my worst year had been the year I got meningitis, at the age of 13; and post 1996, the most challenging year has been this, 2020, the year of the pandemic. 1996 is the pivot. Maybe that's why the year is playing so prominently in my mind. The human mind, when stretched by extenuating circumstances, tends to throw curve balls at us when we least want or need them. We've got to hit them out of the park!

Day 44

3 May 2020

Lockdown 3.0 has come into effect, as the government has decided to keep India closed till 17 May. The map has been divided into red, orange and green zones; the red zones are the hotspots, the orange zones have clusters with few cases, and the green zones correspond to the districts that haven't had a new case in 21 days. Relaxations in the lockdown will be made according to the category of the zone. It's an extremely bureaucratic system to implement, one that can get confusing for an unlettered person, of which there are many. In my opinion, it's wishful thinking to expect an unruly population like ours to abide by such nuanced rules. Given the statistics, however, I go blank when I try to think of an alternate method to control the spread of the virus. The choices are bleak—death by starvation or death by disease. *The administration is consulting the experts; they will choose the best course of action*; it helps when I hear my inner voice speak with such optimism.

The weather is warming up. This Sunday, we ate in my parents' dining room, with the air conditioner on, and not at the *Hawa Mahal*. My aunt joined us for the first time since the beginning of the first lockdown. My father and his sister are both doing better after their brief, albeit intensive, battles with cancer. We discussed the tributes paid by the Indian Armed Forces to the frontline warriors combating the virus. The drill started at 10:00 am with a MiG-29, Sukhoi-30 MKI and Jaguar flying over the Rajpath and then orbiting the capital for 30 minutes. The Air Force conducted fly-pasts by fighter jets over cities and towns across the nation. Military bands played patriotic tunes outside civil hospitals treating patients with the virus. Helicopters showered petals on the hospitals. Tonight, the Western Command will light up five naval ships off the Gateway of India. They'll display banners commending the warriors, fire flares and sound their sirens. Naval ships will light up in Kochi, Visakhapatnam and a number of other coastal towns. The naval air station at Goa will create a human chain on the runway. We questioned if all of this was necessary. Shouldn't the funds that went into these grandiose gestures have gone into actually fighting the virus? The frontline workers got the intended boost in morale, of course, but I believe the migrant workers also deserved to be acknowledged in the tributes. They didn't choose to lose their jobs. They didn't choose to watch their children starve. They were given no choice but to walk hundreds of miles back to their villages from the cities. The government has woken up, at long last, to their plight; they've arranged trains to transport several of them home. But in some states, the migrants are being charged for the journey. In Gujarat, they were charged 780 rupees for a ticket. These are people who haven't eaten for days. They don't have a rupee in their pockets. Another group that warranted a mention in the tributes are the farmers. They didn't choose to grow bumper crops and then watch them waste away in the fields. The families of the victims of the disease, too, deserved a nod, for having to quietly bury their relatives, or receive them as bags of ashes, sometimes, not even that. The money spent on military bands, fly-pasts, illuminating naval ships and on helicopters showering rose petals over hospitals could have been spent on getting the migrants home, free of cost, and feeding and sheltering those who are still stranded alongside train tracks and highways. Zoological parks and wildlife rescue centres, that are currently in dire need, could have availed of those funds to feed their animals. I'm sure the frontline workers wouldn't have minded the money going into assisting the helpless and the needy.

Mehrauli has been declared a red zone. We are now in a containment area.

Day 45

4 May 2020

Putra moh. The closest translation of this term in English is the love for one's son. Why I say "closest" is because *putra moh* goes beyond the unconditional love a parent feels for his or her son; it alludes to a love that verges on infatuation. The blinding nature of infatuation makes this love an almost irrational kind of love. Young women of foreign origin, who marry Indian men and relocate to the country, are not immune to this infectious sentiment either. Leaders of the biggest opposition parties in our country have been accused of it. My mother, I can say from personal experience, fell prey to it. My brother is a man of leisure and I'm a writer and a housewife, neither of us manage to run our homes entirely on our own; yet my brother lives with negligible financial stress, and I, well, I live with a significant amount of it. Those that muster the courage and ask my mother, "Why for son and not for daughter?" receive the prompt reply, "Because her husband should be providing for her." This, coming from a woman who was born in the Netherlands and raised in the US, proves the mesmeric, contagious power of *putra moh.*

When a poor woman in India gives birth to twins, a male and a female, the male child, it has been observed, gets to drink his fill of his mother's milk before the female is offered a breast to latch on to. What helps the female survive, under such circumstances, is her superior immunity. The fight for equality in the workplace began a long time ago. But what about the hardest battle of all—the one at home? That's a different kind of battle altogether, fought by an outnumbered woman behind the closed doors and windows of her home. And though she may be aware that she is not alone in fighting it—there are others fighting elsewhere, behind their own closed doors and windows—it's still a desperately lonely battle.

Arjuna, the great warrior from the Mahabharata, got weak when he saw his teachers and relatives on the battlefield. Dropping to the floor of his chariot, he told his charioteer that he couldn't get himself to fight them. Lord Krishna, who was the charioteer, told him that it wasn't his relatives he was fighting: he was fighting for what was right. Life is the battlefield, he said, and the battle is between right and wrong. The charioteer here symbolises our overarching higher self, also known as God. We must listen to the voice of reason present within each one of us and follow its guidance—that is the basic premise of the *Gita*. It is so much easier to sit on the sidelines and say, "I'm okay with letting it go. I can do without. I don't mind losing. It takes too much energy to fight. I don't want my relationships to get messy. I'd rather walk away." Not taking a stand is also a choice. The one who chooses not to take a stand, according to the doctrine of reincarnation, has to go through numerous births to understand that forward movement can only happen when one takes a stand; and if the stand requires a fight, then one must fight. There are numerous myths in the Hindu tradition that shed light on this philosophical assumption. The battle between Raktabija and Goddess Kali is one of them. Raktabija was causing havoc in the heavens and on earth. None of the gods could defeat him, no matter how hard they tried, because from every drop of his blood that fell to the ground, another Raktabija emerged. With his clones multiplying and fighting beside him, the demon, it seemed, was invincible. The gods turned to Kali, as they usually do in extreme situations. She descended with diabolical energy upon the battlefield and launched a quicksilver attack on the replicating clones. The battle went on and on until it occurred to Kali that the only way to destroy the demon was to swallow his blood before it fell to the ground. As she slayed the clones, she drank their blood, until every last demon was gone. Raktabija, like the charioteer in the Mahabharata, is a metaphor. He represents our human frailties. When we conquer one destructive habit, be it a manner of thinking, behaving, or harming ourselves by not standing up for ourselves, we notice another habit that we hadn't noticed before or that recently developed. In order to achieve perfection, we have to keep fighting our limiting tendencies, defeating one bad habit after another. Very few can do it in one life. When we finally reach perfection, we are released from the cycle of repeated births—we get what is known as moksha. The people we revere the most in society, the sages and saints, remarkable world leaders like Nelson Mandela, Martin Luther King and Gandhi, are the people who've come the closest to controlling their negative tendencies, and by doing so, have gained the respect and adulation of the rest of us mortals.

For me, my sons are equal; I don't favour one over the other. If only daughters and sons, everywhere, were viewed as equals by their parents. I'm trying to muster the courage that Arjuna had, to listen to his charioteer and, gaining confidence and faith, ride into battle. Mine is about achieving fairness at home. Come to think of it, so was Arjuna's.

Day 46

5 May 2020

A professor at Harvard University, Deirdre Barrett has conducted a study on Post Traumatic Nightmares. Barrett recorded the dreams of 5,000 volunteers and found that the anxiety the pandemic is causing in people is making them have similar dreams. It is the first time the phenomenon has occurred since the bombing of Hiroshima and Nagasaki; the fear of radiation in the survivors gave them nightmares of getting burns or radiation sickness. Post Traumatic Nightmares were also experienced by Holocaust survivors. More recently, the phenomenon was recorded after 9/11.

A sense of uncertainty about the future and the fear of contracting the virus is causing people to have vivid dreams of bugs, or of being infected and unable to breathe. People living alone have been dreaming that they're in prison or isolated from other humans in some way.

I experienced this phenomenon of shared dreaming after an upsetting event in my own life. It was when I was at boarding school. I was getting ready to go for breakfast when a friend of mine entered the room and told me that Rajiv Gandhi had died. She had heard it from the bearers in the cafeteria. I rushed to the TV lounge in the dormitory to watch Doordarshan and learn if it was true. As the report rolled on, I was shocked to find that the man I called Rajiv uncle was gone. I thought about his family and also my father. How inconsolable they must be!

In English class the next day, I couldn't hold back my tears and had to be taken to the teachers' lounge. It was when I was reading a poem by Wilfred Owen—we were studying war poetry—when I broke down. It was the poem, *Mental Cases*:

Who are these? Why sit they here in twilight?
Wherefore rock they, purgatorial shadows,
Drooping tongues from jaws that slob their relish,
Baring teeth that leer like skulls' teeth wicked?
Stroke on stroke of pain, —but what slow panic,
Gouged these chasms round their fretted sockets?
Ever from their hair and through their hands' palms
Misery swelters. Surely we have perished
Sleeping, and walk hell; but who these hellish?

—These are men whose minds the Dead have ravished.
Memory fingers in their hair of murders,
Multitudinous murders they once witnessed.
Wading sloughs of flesh these helpless wander,
Treading blood from lungs that had loved laughter.
Always they must see these things and hear them,
Batter of guns and shatter of flying muscles,
Carnage incomparable and human squander
Rucked too thick for these men's extrication.

Therefore still their eyeballs shrink tormented
Back into their brains, because on their sense

Sunlight seems a blood-smear; night comes blood-black;
Dawn breaks open like a wound that bleeds afresh.
—Thus their heads wear this hilarious, hideous,
Awful falseness of set-smiling corpses.
—Thus their hands are plucking at each other;
Picking at the rope-knouts of their scourging;
Snatching after us who smote them, brother,
Pawing us who dealt them war and madness.

Then began the dreaming. The first was a warning dream—I'm warning Rajiv Gandhi that something bad is going to happen. He's walking in his white kurta-pyjama in the Lodhi Gardens, trailed by a gaggle of party workers. I see that there is a slush pool in his path. "Rajiv uncle, don't go there," I warned him. In the next dream I have of him, I'm sitting in my classroom when he comes through the door, wearing a black cardigan. Surprised to see him at school, I got up and went to him. He raises his hands, the palms facing me, and smiles. I join my palms to his, and as I do so, his sweater begins to turn yellow; the colour grows and grows until it forms an aura around him. In yet another dream, I see Rajiv uncle on a mountain covered with snow. I call out to him, though my lips aren't moving: it is as if my mind is calling out to him. He turns and looks at me and then walks on. In my last dream of him, I'm sitting on the wing of a 6-seater airplane, the kind I sometimes went up in with my father. Rajiv uncle was flying it. He peers out from the pilot's window and smiles at me. He had a sweet smile in life. Feeling reassured, I smile back at him. This was a happy dream. It showed acceptance, on my part, that he was gone.

The dreams impacted me so strongly that I had to share them with someone who was close to the man. I decided to write a letter to his daughter. I felt that, if I was experiencing such strong emotions, she must surely be experiencing something similar. A few days after sending the letter, I got a reply. She shared with me that the dreams she had had of her father, subsequent to his death, were similar in nature to mine. In a letter seven-pages long, written in smooth flowing prose, she described her dreams to me. Our dreams were uncannily similar. This was the first, and only, time I experienced the phenomenon of shared dreaming.

On a lighter note, I feel compelled to share here the goofy dream I had the night I watched the segment on CNN about the kinds of Post Traumatic Nightmares people are having. I dreamt that a Tyrannosaurus Rex was chasing me, a massive and remarkably ugly bug!

Day 47

6 May 2020

62 trains have transported 75,000 migrants back to their home states. It is feared that many of them are carrying the virus. The travellers will be quarantined for 14 days before they're allowed to enter their villages. I'm praying the disease doesn't spread deep into rural India; medical facilities there are close to non-existent. While migrants are lining up at train stations, city folk are lining up outside liquor stores. Several cities have allowed shops to reopen. When interviewed about the inconvenience citizens were willing to endure to buy alcohol, a retired colonel, crammed like a matchstick in a matchbox between customers standing outside a store, said it was totally worth it to get the "liquid gold". The police have had to resort to lathi-charge in several areas to get patrons to stand 1 m apart. The social distancing measures stretched the lines a kilometre long. It was a comical sight to behold—comic relief in gloomy times.

Spring left a bounty of new monkeys in the garden. There are babies and mothers everywhere, all hanging out like at a birthday party. Macaques are attentive mothers. I was watching one of them caring for her baby. Picking seeds off the ground, she was acutely aware of the infant who kept trying to hop away from her to explore its surroundings. It was a male—I saw his seed-sized testicles. When he went too far for comfort, which was no further than 2 feet, she would take him in her arms and press him against her breast. The baby suckled for a while and then tried going off again; but the vigilant mother grabbed him by the leg and pulled him back to her. Monkey life is in full swing. Alliances are being made, fights are being fought over territory between rival gangs, and mothers are running around with babies latched to their underbellies or backs, breastfeeding or snoozing, and, needless to say, dropping monkey poop everywhere.

Suraj Singh has managed to get chlorine for the swimming pool. He's been on the job like a fly on monkey poo to get the chemical the lockdowns made near-impossible to source. We have enough now to last us three months. The Man Friday goes to extremes to prove his indispensability—that's how he's had such lasting power. He gets the job done, by hook or by crook. It is this resourcefulness that convinced my mother of his indispensability. (I personally believe no employee is indispensable, but who am I to say that?) Anyhow, I couldn't be happier that the chlorine has arrived. To swim, what a luxury!

Day 48

7 May 2020

Bollywood said goodbye to two of its finest actors last week, Rishi Kapoor and Irfan Khan. The former was a character as grand on screen as in real life. His career spanned half a century. The latter was an extraordinarily versatile actor, a man who'll be remembered as much for the courage with which he embraced his untimely death from cancer as his outstanding performances.

My first flight in a helicopter was with an actor, Amitabh Bachchan. His daughter, Shweta, and I were friends around the time we were 12. She invited me to join her family in Ooty, where her father was shooting for a movie, *Shahenshah*.

Amit uncle took us to a Chinese restaurant on the evening I arrived in Mumbai. It was my first time in the city and first attempt at using chopsticks. That night, I had a tormenting ache in my stomach, and by morning, I had diarrhoea. Unbeknownst to me, a hostile bacterium had hitched an unwelcome ride on my chopsticks to my tummy. Jaya auntie gave me a pill to calm my system down. It got me to Ooty without an incident. But, once again, at nightfall, my stomach gave way, and this time, it was worse; I had to wash my underpants before anyone woke up and hang them up to dry in the bathroom us girls were sharing!

I had many firsts on this trip. I'd never been on a film set. It was far from what I knew of my world of politics. Filmmaking was something else altogether; it was sheer creativity; it was fantastic.

I watched the actress, Meenakshi Sheshadri, roll down a verdant hill, wearing make-up, high heels and a flouncy dress, over and over again, until the director was satisfied with the shot. I heard the song they were picturising in Ooty so many times that I can never forget it. (*Jaane do, jaane do, mujhe jaana hai. Vaada jo kiya hai woh nibhana hai.*) I would pull up my plastic chair and sit next to Meenakshi Sheshadri on location every day. She was friendly, and smiled a lot; I liked that. She sailed through her gruelling schedules without complaint. Her work ethic was inspiring.

Mr Bachchan required white shoes to match the trousers he was wearing for the song sequence. The costume department hadn't managed to arrange them for him, and so the director removed his own white leather shoes, which he happened to be wearing, coincidently, and gave them to Mr Bachchan. For the rest of the day, the director worked in his socks; the shoes of the actor destined to become so renowned in his later years that he would simply be called Big B, were too hallowed for the director to put on his inferior, and, possibly smelly, feet.

There was a dinner at the hotel, which Shashi Kapoor's son, Karan, attended. The young man had just started his modelling career. He seemed so familiar to me, perhaps because he was a half-breed like myself. As I watched Shweta and Karan dance after the dinner, I wondered if I should go up to him and introduce myself, at some point, but I was so mortified by the possibility of my stomach causing a far-from-pleasant incident, I didn't move from my self-appointed corner.

Shweta's brother, Abhishek, was also with his family in Ooty. Compared to my brother and his friend Rahul—they were the boys I hung out with in Delhi, always up to mischief, like playing impish pranks, dunking me in the pool and shooting pellets at the crows—Abhishek was so polite that it seemed as if he was born well-mannered. Like many active and athletic kids, Rahul gave himself a proper scar—a dimple on his left cheek—from an arrow let loose from a crossbow he got as a gift. My brother, too, has a scar, from where matches in his pocket rubbed against each other and caught fire. Rather surprisingly, nonetheless, in adulthood, the two buds became especially composed versions of their former selves. Too composed, almost.

Despite the fact that my stomach was upset for most of my holiday with the Bachchan family, the fascination I developed with filmmaking on that trip, stayed: it is no coincidence that I ended up marrying an actor.

Day 49

8 May 2020

As the global death toll surpasses 270,000, the pandemic continues to unleash horrors; one in five children in America are not getting enough food; in Mumbai's Sion Hospital, the dead lie, wrapped in plastic bags, on beds, beside the living; a train mowed down 16 migrants as they slept, exhausted and hungry, on the tracks in Aurangabad.

In the biggest evacuation plan since Indian Independence, 64 flights have been arranged by the government to bring back citizens stranded abroad. The 14,800 evacuees returning to the homeland will be quarantined for 14 days upon arrival.

Vegetable vendors are the latest super spreaders of the virus in Ahmedabad. Only chemist and milk shops will be open till 15 May. The paramilitary has been deployed in the city to impose a stringent lockdown.

Day 50

9 May 2020

"Why doesn't the government invest in rural areas so that villagers don't have to migrate to the cities to find jobs?" It's a question I've heard people ask often. I was one of them, once.

I joined my father on the campaign trail when he contested elections from Rae Bareli in 1999. I'd returned from college just a year before, educated in American work ethics, soft, guileless, ill-prepared for what I was going to encounter: abject poverty. I spent one month in Rae Bareli, driven in beat-up jeeps on dirt roads, from village to village, to ask people for their votes. Some of the villages were like ghost towns; children, grossly outnumbering the adults, coming out in droves to receive our motorcade. I walked in alleys obstructed by stinking puddles teeming with mosquitoes. I encountered old widows roaming the villages in torn white saris becoming brown, forced to beg to survive, their eyes haunting me with their hopelessness. Young mothers shoved babies with limbs grotesquely twisted by polio at me, crying, "Do something, please, do something." These were the innocent. This was where they lived. After meeting them, it was hard for me to come by anyone innocent again in the city where I lived. They were the written-off people.

I felt embarrassed asking them for their votes. I felt embarrassed asking them for anything; because I couldn't make them a promise that I wasn't sure I could keep. I was confident, my father, as their representative in the parliament, would do what he could for them, but I couldn't give them my word for it. I'd badger my father at the end of each day with questions like, "Why aren't there enough schools here? Why is there just one hospital? Why isn't there work for them? Why aren't there mills and factories here?" Everywhere I went, the men would tell me they were jobless: they wanted work.

Reflecting upon those days from the midst of this humanitarian crisis has given me the answers to those questions. There is an unwritten policy, shared by all political parties, that makes every successive party coming to power tow the same line. The policy is to invest in urban centres, where the rich and the brains of the machine live. The nuts and bolts of the machine are imported from the villages. The migrant workers, the nuts and bolts, live in the slums and toil to build the cities for the rich. The powers that be reckon that the locals won't work for such low wages and under such despicable conditions, for as long hours as the villagers will, if given no choice. If the villagers had adequate hospitals and employment opportunities back home, why would they migrate to the cities to do their dirty work, leaving behind their wives, parents and children? This migrant crisis we are seeing wouldn't have happened if the locals were given reasonable wages to work in construction and sanitation and every other essential profession that is largely, and wrongly, considered menial.

The questions of my youth answered, I have but one question now: "Mr Prime Minister, how exactly will you achieve your goal of 'Make in India' if you don't build factories and mills in rural districts?"

Day 51

10 May 2020

My parents gave the name of a short general with a big ego to a large dog with an even bigger ego—Napoleon. It was when we moved from Panchsheel Park to Greater Kailash that we got our first Great Dane. The gunmetal grey dog became infamous in E-Block, not only for his size but also his temperament.

When I took Napoleon for a round of the park, once, it so happened that a toddler and his maid were walking in front of us. The child was jumping up and down, and I could tell that this was bugging the dog. I was barely a teenager at the time, my wits were not about me, and so I didn't act upon the signal my mild nervousness was giving me. Napoleon lunged forward and snapped at the boy. The boy started running, and, as he did, his sweater began unravelling; a string from the sweater had caught in Napoleon's teeth. I cut the string loose and hurried back home from the opposite direction. Not fifteen minutes later, the boy and his entire family, including the grandmother who had knitted the sweater, were at our gate. I hid on the rooftop—the same rooftop where my father had taught me how to whistle like a man. Everyone was searching for me to know what had happened. Cowering like a child, I peered over the side of the roof at the assemblage at the gate. I felt sorry for the boy, who I knew would never forget the incident and was likely to be afraid of dogs for the rest of his life, and for the grandmother who had lovingly knitted the sweater with her, likely, arthritic hands. I noticed that the lower half of the garment was gone; what the boy was now wearing, in today's lingo, was a crop top. If only his family would have known, in the not-too-distant future, crop tops would become all the rage!

A week had passed since the incident with the sweater, when a swami visited our house. I was instructed by my grandmother to give him company until my father could join him. When I got to the living room, I saw that the guest already had company—Napoleon. The swami was tall, dark and broad, with a bushy beard, and salt and pepper hair to his shoulders; he had a formidable presence. Over his white robes, he wore a *mala* with the biggest *rudraksha* beads my 13-year-old eyes had ever seen. The beads were linked with clasps of gold. The *tilak* on his forehead was a fiery orange—blinding, potentially hypnotic. To Napoleon, though, it was all a lot of hocus-pocus. He greeted the swami by pinning him against the wall and sticking his nose under his *lungi*. I learned, later on, that this was no ordinary swami—this was Chandraswami; spiritual advisor to the Sultan of Brunei, Elizabeth Taylor, Margaret Thatcher, the King of Jordan, Hosni Mubarak, tennis player, John McEnroe, and the arms dealer, Adnan Khashoggi. He had predicted to Margaret Thatcher that she would become the Prime Minister of the United Kingdom, and when she did, the two became lifelong friends. The swami travelled on private jets and luxurious yachts. To Napoleon, it was of no consequence, none of it: he was interested only in what was under the swami's silken *lungi*. Chandraswami, it appeared, had, alas, met his match in an equally nosy, swaggering, notorious being. I yanked Napoleon by his collar and pulled him away from the god-man—the first god-man to give a whole new twist to the term "god-man".

Both Chandraswami and my father were raised in Hyderabad. Though neither were native Hyderabadis—the swami was Rajasthani and my father Punjabi—they both spoke fluent Telugu. They had met through a mutual friend, Narasimha Rao. After his encounter with Napoleon, the swami didn't come to our house again, but he did send an enticing gift to the farm for my father, of which I shall write in my next entry.

The swami was suspected, by the Jain Commission, of being involved in the plot to assassinate Rajiv Gandhi. It was likely a financial involvement, they said. The Commission needed names; mighty names, sellable names, disposable names. My father didn't buy the allegation; in his view, Chandraswami was an easy scapegoat. The sad fact is that a lot of people wanted Rajiv Gandhi dead: the Sikh militants, the Kashmiri extremists, the LTTE and Pakistan's ISI (who want every Indian Prime Minister dead!). Whether the assassination was planned in cahoots by the vested interests or solely by the LTTE, no one will know, not until new evidence is unearthed. Individuals with ties to international players may have had an inkling of the hatching plot but with no part to play in it. I'm certain such individuals regretted not raising an alarm when they had the chance. The likeliest theory, according to me, is that the LTTE, along with Tamil Nadu state players, were responsible for it. The Jain Commission clearly stated that the DMK provided sanctuary to the rebels who planned and carried out the assassination.

On one of the rare occasions my father took me to Chandraswami's ashram, the swami told me about his latest pilgrimage to Vaishno Devi. Noticing that he had lost a lot of weight, I asked him, "What is your secret?" He was climbing up the hill to the shrine, he said, when it started raining. His followers told him about a cave where they could take refuge. The sadhu residing in the cave welcomed the group and gave them shelter for the night. The cave-dwelling sanyasi told Chandraswami that it wasn't healthy for him to be so heavy. He gave him some special leaves from a tree on the hillside and told him to swallow two leaves with hot water, every morning and evening, for a month. About the time he was taking the leaves, Chandraswami said, "Mai roz subah itni latrine karta tha," indicating with his hands an amount equivalent to the size of a football. The description made me promptly ditch the idea of asking him to get me the leaves so I, too, could lose the weight I had gained consequent to motherhood. It was genuinely scary—the thought of pushing out that much poop every morning. The swami, however, took pride in it; he boasted about it as if it was a phenomenal feat.

I invited Chandraswami to the farm for Sunday lunch, not only because he was an old buddy of my father's, but also because I was intrigued by the man. I have a character based on him in my first book. Chandraswami was a Tantrik, astrologer and mind reader; people feared gazing into his eyes, for fear of being read or hypnotised by him; but when I looked into his eyes, I saw an inquisitive child; an inquisitive, and equally shrewd and manipulative, child.

The swami was happy to come to lunch. I think he was aware that he didn't have much time; his kidneys were failing. He was at the hospital every third day, for dialysis. When he was leaving, after lunch, I gave him a bottle of pain-relieving oil for his feet. He was deeply touched by the gesture. On his last trip abroad, to Russia, he brought back two bottles of Beluga Vodka for me. He gave them to me, saying, "*Aap sakshat Kali ho.*" I felt more than a pang of pride to be called Kali. I knew that, for a man like him, who neither praised people nor cared for praise, it was a huge compliment. It was my turn to be touched.

Chandraswami died the same year.

Day 52

11 May 2020

The gift Chandraswami sent to the farm for my father reminded me of the British actress, Liz Hurley. She was fashionable, intelligent and eloquent. She had impeccable manners. She was an Oxford graduate. She was also a high-class call girl.

It must have come as a surprise to her that the politician she had come to serve received her at his home with his wife and children. After lunch with the family in the *Hawa Mahal*, my mother took her around the farm to show her the vegetables and fruit trees. I doubt she'd ever had an experience like this on any of her assignments!

That was Chandraswami's first and last attempt at getting Capt. Satish Sharma into the palm of his hand—the hand that played magic tricks and made politicians, actresses, athletes and arms dealers his flock. From that day forth, my father and the swami became friends.

He didn't talk much, this swami; listening and witchery made him friends with the powerful and super-rich, and sending enticing gifts. The man had a personality; all else can be denied about him, but not this. How boring the world would be without the likes of Chandraswami!

Day 53

12 May 2020

The Prime Minister has declared a 20 lakh crore package to help small businesses, infrastructure, migrants and farmers. It is the fifth-largest relief package after nations like Germany and Japan. The challenge will be how this money reaches the intended destinations; there should be no room for middlemen. The Indian Prime Minister says he envisions a "quantum jump" in how our systems operate, in regards to transparency and efficiency. If he indeed achieves what he says he intends to, Swami Vivekananda's prediction of India becoming a superpower will become a reality.

Day 54

13 May 2020

The global food industry is one machine that needs an overhaul. The pandemic is forcing us to re-evaluate systems that are detrimental to the planet and also to us as human beings. We're realising that we have to bring change if we wish for a sustainable future. Epidemics will come, pandemics even, but are we okay with them causing the loss of trillions of dollars to the global economy? Are we okay with them rendering us jobless, homeless and hungry? If we don't change certain key systems of living, there will be a repeat of what is happening now, in the next pandemic.

According to the United Nations' Food and Agriculture Organisation (FAO), 815 million people suffered from chronic undernourishment in 2016. This, while up to 40% of the food produced globally was wasted. 80 billion land animals are slaughtered each year to feed 7.6 billion people. The industrial farms, where these animals are raised and butchered, are largely "wet", like the Wuhan market, where the pandemic allegedly began. These farms are hotspots for viruses. Not only do the animals at these facilities suffer inhumane conditions but the workers, who are mostly migrants, do too. They work in a highly unsafe environment for low wages. The work is fast-paced and, if the employees are sick, they are refused days off from work. How can anyone say slavery is abolished in view of these facts?

We need a change in the production, distribution and consumption of food. To create a sustainable and safe food culture, we'll have to limit the operations of meat farms and increase the cost of meat. Efficient local and regional production of meat, or other food sources, should be the way to go. Experimentation with artificial meat is leading to alternate sources of protein: with further investment, this can, for many, be a satisfying replacement for real meat derived from live animals. Some people may choose vegetarianism as a safer and more environmentally friendly option. The night I saw Fareed Zakaria on GPS give the figure of 80 billion as the number of land animals we eat each year, I couldn't sleep. The figure floated around in my head and damaged a portion of my brain. Like dark matter, it's made an uncomfortable space for itself in my consciousness.

Food for thought: If we eat 80 billion land animals every year, how many sea creatures must we be eating?

Day 55

14 May 2020

I dreamt that I was in an airplane that took off from a road between high-rise buildings. The pilot is confident that he can get the plane to ascend, but it doesn't; it flies level with the top floors of the towering office blocks. They are too close for comfort; I look out of my window at them with a sense of dread. The pilot with the salt and pepper hair pulls the throttle, but it makes no difference; the plane continues to fly level with the buildings. The passengers, 80 in all, are apprehensive. The pilot communicates with the control tower until he loses radio connectivity. The airplane falters, and then drops on its belly upon the road. We climb out of the broken craft and wander the derelict parks and deserted stores, waiting for rescue vehicles that never arrive. Without a plan, we roam, we wait, aimless.

Day 56

15 May 2020

The wind filled the air with the red flowers of Goldmohur trees, yellow Neem leaves, the emerald leaves of the Peepul, dandelions and dust. I stood like a snowman in a blizzard, my dressing gown ballooning into an umbrella. It seemed the storm would lift me up, up and up, through the swirling flowers and leaves, dandelions and dust. A breaking, ripping sound—and a tall tree fell. I went back inside the house and changed into my swimwear; I had to take part in this weather event. The wind died down by the time I returned; storms in Delhi aren't like the ones in Mumbai—long and wet. The storm had come alone, without a drop of rain.

The pool was a blue painting with a floral frame. I waded in, removing twigs fallen from the Peepul, and came across a hoverfly caught in a miniature whirlpool. Along with the flowers, leaves, dandelions and dust, the hoverfly had been blown about by the tempest. I lifted it out of the waters with a leaf and set it on the side of the pool. After resting for a while, it began drying its wings with its spindly legs. It lifted its rear and rubbed its hind legs over the length of its body.

Birds started singing, and the monkeys huddled on the walls became active. The young ones discovered the broken tree lying on the smaller trees beside it, making a bridge parallel to the boundary wall. They investigated this new feature in their territory, cautiously, at first, and then, rambunctiously. They ran along the length of the fallen giant, playing catch, plunging into the bushes and then climbing back onto the horizontal branches. The storm had gifted them a jungle gym. I turned to look at the hoverfly. Rested and satisfied with its dryness, it had flown away.

Today was a day as good as a day can get—pandemic or not.

Day 57

16 May 2020

Waving his arms in the air, complaining that his brother was "clingy" and "irritating", Robin bumped into my laptop and sent it crashing to the ground. It stopped working. After days of making frantic phone calls, I got a computer technician to come to the farm. He took it away with him.

Bereft of my computer, I swam for three hours, baked cakes and cookies, daydreamed, read in the lawn and watched the children thrash each other on the PlayStation. Thankfully, I was rewarded for spending as much time as I did with the boys; Robin made me a video on Mother's Day. He selected pictures of me with his father, friends and family, from my phonebook, and put them together in a video with captions that read: "This is Sharika", "She is a loving family member", "And a friend", "And she is a fun person to hang out with", "She is an all-star", "Happy Mother's Day", "Love, Robin". The captions popped up between photos, on lined paper with a bouncing ball and a jumping burger. He layered the video with music and end titles. It was remarkably well done, even if I say it, his mother.

I wrote on paper until I got my computer back, and now that it's here, my fingers are tapping on the keyboard like a tap dancer dancing after getting new shoes, to a pianist playing after a long deprivation of her piano. I have so much to say; all writers do. Writers *have* to write, or they'll explode. Or implode. Don't know which, but it's definitely one of the two.

Day 58

17 May 2020

I've been noticing the distance between my husband and I growing; and it's not just the 1,436 km separating us that's responsible for it, but also that we have less and less in common; he is living his life and we're living ours.

I watch monkeys springing off the branches of a tree and into the deep end of the pool. They dive underwater and pop up in the shallow, their strokes effortless and swift. I enjoy watching the monkeys, but since they've bitten two people in the span of ten days, my sentiments towards them are not as warm as usual. I had to buy rabies shots and get my aunt, who used to be a doctor, to administer them to the victims— the guard at the gate and a gardener. While I was swimming yesterday, a big monkey, possibly an alpha male, ran towards me and threatened to dive into the water. Females and their infants were on a wall nearby; he may have been trying to protect them, or show off to them. Sitting on the side of the pool, watching this ball with eyes, hair and a mouth full of teeth bobbing towards him, could also have triggered the aggressive reaction.

My children's behaviour has been almost as bad as that of the monkeys. Robin has ADHD and dyslexia. Children like him need a routine. The pandemic has tossed all that out. Implementing a new routine has been no mean feat. When the school complained that Robin was not paying attention during his online classes, I became more vigilant and got to know that he was sneakily watching YouTube videos on the phone. When I confiscated the phone during school hours, he got into the habit of switching off his camera to go for a toilet break, an ice tea in the kitchen, and a spin on his bicycle. It's impossible for me to sit with the children from 8.30 a.m. to 3 p.m. to ensure that they're attending their online classes; I have other work to do. I've been checking on them, unannounced, every hour, since the complaint. Unable to meet other 12 year olds like himself, in a state of perpetual enclosure, is frustrating my elder son; he vents by going into a hyperactive fit, waving his arms and shrieking; that's when the demolitions happened, of the computer and a wall-hanging clock. The MacBook Pro took 48,000 rupees to fix—a cost that pinched me as hard as the effort it took to get a technician to come to the house, since electronics shops are still closed.

Meanwhile, the farcical Sunday lunches continue. My sister-in-law praises my mother over lunch, while, in the rest of the week, dishes delectable tales about "the old MIL" to friends. The two husbands, my father and brother, remain fixed to their seats, motionless: when the women say "Up," like soldiers they respond to the command, when they say, "Sit," they remain as they are, and when the women wish them to stay silent, no command is necessary, just a sharp glance suffices. I sit across from my aunt, the two nobodies at the table, and bide the time. It's like everything's on Repeat mode. The wasps clinging to the tendrils of the plants in the day, mildly buzzing, the rise in the number of diseased, worldwide, now at 5 million, the children's misbehaviour, the aggression of the monkeys, the farcical Sunday lunches: it's the same, week after week. Time is going in circles. Even the news is on Repeat mode; there's only the news of the virus on every channel, every day—only the news of the virus. I may not have the virus but the virus has gotten to me.

"To-morrow, and to-morrow, and to-morrow, creeps in this petty pace from day to day, to the last syllable of recorded time." (*Macbeth*, Act 5, Scene 5)

Day 59

18 May 2020

When the astronauts at the International Space Station look upon earth from their solitary abode, it appears the same as it always has. So deceptive is this disease, this invisible foe, silently spreading its invincible tentacles across the planet.

The Pentagon recently released videos of unidentified flying objects, shot by navy fighter pilots engaged in drills off the Pacific coast. The release of the videos rekindled the public's interest in the phenomenon of UFOs and the debate on the existence of alien life. The notion that earth is the only planet with life, to me, is absurd. Everything on earth, indeed, in the universe, came from the atoms from an exploding star billions of years ago. The ingredients of life are out there in the universe, same as they are here on earth, so why wouldn't there be life outside our solar system? The astronomer, Frank Drake, devised an equation by which to estimate the number of planets with conditions suitable to support intelligent life in the universe. When this mathematical equation was implemented, many years later, it revealed that there were hundreds of thousands of planets that technically could support intelligent life. So why are we so arrogant to believe that we are the only intelligent life forms in space—a space so infinite that light from the Big Bang that took place 13.8 billion years ago still hasn't reached us? Since we can't see the edge of the universe, we can't decisively say that there *is* one. In ancient times, people believed the earth was flat because they couldn't see further than the horizon; that belief was busted when eastern astronomers, and then the Greeks, declared that the earth was spherical. The universe could be spherical. It could be infinite. There could be parallel universes. The story of the universe, and of us, is still unfolding.

We don't know why ancient Sanskrit scrolls and cave paintings depict alien life forms. The Book of Ezekiel mentions a sighting of an extraterrestrial life form. Pharaoh Akhenaten had an elongated skull, similar to the skulls found in Peru, dating back to 300 bc. In the 15th-century painting, "The Madonna with Saint Giovannino", there's a depiction of a man and his dog, looking up at a flying object. There were no aircrafts, balloons, or flying objects of any kind, at the time: the depiction could only have ensued from the painter's imagination or from having witnessed such an object or from listening to a narration of a sighting. There have been numerous unsolved sightings involving groups of hundreds of people. Buzz Aldrin has spoken of seeing something flying alongside the shuttle while on board the Apollo 11, the flight that landed humans on the moon. US President, Jimmy Carter, described his own alien encounter. Bill Clinton admitted being denied access to classified information on extraterrestrial encounters; this led many to believe that governments have intentionally covered up compelling evidence of the existence of extraterrestrial life forms. The public is denied the facts.

Extraterrestrials have been watching us. According to thousands of accounts, over the span of decades, they have abducted and probed us. We can decide for ourselves how likely it is that these thousands of people experienced a collective hallucination. Extraterrestrials have walked amongst us—how else did the elongated skulls discovered by archaeologists in Peru make their way to earth? Assuming that they do keep tabs on us, must they be knowing about the scourge humanity has brought upon itself? Do they see, with their super-advanced spy technology, the mass graves dug in Iran and Brazil, and the bodies wrapped in sheets and lying on the streets in Ecuador? They see the lights turned down on this otherwise shimmering, glitzy planet. They notice the tall vents of factories have stopped spewing hazardous smoke into the atmosphere. They see the seizing of air traffic, vehicular activity, shipping, and the bombings in Yemen and Syria. It's possible they're wondering why humans aren't acting their normal selves. They may already have snapped up some unassuming soul taking a walk at night somewhere in Greenland, or teleported a dead body off a street in Ecuador, and conducted examinations on it to find out what on earth was going on. Humans. Stupid humans. How stupid they must think us to be. No wonder the Grays managed to advance so far—no longer needing big mouths for sustenance and hair for protection, consuming small quantities of ethically grown superfoods, communicating telepathically. Humans are such comical, primitive beings, in comparison; so caught up in ego: their love for themselves takes them two steps forward and ten steps back. The extraterrestrials have probably always known what goes on here but decided we were too dumb to deserve their guidance or help. Our response to an encounter would likely be to blow their spaceship up the first chance we get; we're so fearful of the foreign, the dissimilar—so suspicious and defensive.

I'm glad we're being watched by a big brother entity, even if it's just being watched and not guided. The watchers are benevolent towards us; if they weren't, they would have blown us up by now or invaded our planet and taken over. They watch. And they wait. They wait until we're mature enough to accept them with a measure of benevolence. I'm guessing they're going to have to wait a long time; for as long as we have world leaders like Xi Jinping, Bashar al-Assad, Kim Jong-un, Jair Bolsonaro and Donald Trump, benevolence will remain just a word. Chances are, they'll confuse Donald Trump with Donald Duck. I know I do.

Day 60

19 May 2020

When he was minister for petroleum and natural gas, my father went to China on an official visit. When he was done with the engagements lined up for him over the three-day visit, his Chinese counterpart invited him over to dinner at his house. The men ate, drank, and became friends. When my father returned to India, he brought with him an ornamental Geisha doll in a glass case, and a big cylindrical jar—gifts from the Chinese minister.

My friend, a beautiful girl with a thoroughly inept name, Tunnu, was at my house, as was often the case. We had a swim, watched television, and then got hungry. Searching for food in my mother's kitchen, we came upon the jar wrapped in silken cloth with dragon motifs. Thinking the jar contained exotic Chinese edibles, I unwrapped the cloth, and shuddered on finding nine deadly snakes coiled one on top of the other inside the jar. Most of them had their eyes open, as if staring back at us from their entrapment. Some had their mouths open, too, revealing their fangs. Tunnu dared me to open the jar and sniff the translucent liquid the snakes were preserved in. I cautiously stepped closer, as if the snakes were alive—they certainly looked it—and unscrewed the glass lid. "What are you doing?" came my mother's voice from behind us. We jumped out of our skins (while the snakes still had theirs on). "Um... errr... what is this?" I asked my mother, pointing at the jar. "It's Nine Snake Wine," she replied. Tunnu and I looked at each other, aghast. People actually drank that stuff!

My brother and I had some friends over the same weekend. We ate chips and watched MTV, and, downing a few beers, remembered the Nine Snake Wine. In every group of teenagers, there's always one fat kid and one clown. "I dare you to drink the snake wine," Suveer told Shareef, the clown in our group. Everyone giggled. "I'm not in a suicidal mood today, thank you," Shareef replied. "The snakes have been soaking in vodka for six months—the poison's got neutralised." I nodded in the affirmative when Shareef asked, "Are you sure it's safe to drink it?" I reminded him of how he once downed 100 millilitres of Chinese vinegar with chopped green chillies in it, on a dare.

The five of us snuck into the kitchen after my parents went to bed, and uncovered the jar. What an adrenaline rush we got on seeing the snakes glaring at us with their dead eyes! "You can do it, Sherriff," Tunnu said. We were tipsy, looking for thrills. "We'll all pitch in, 100 rupees a piece, if you do," I told him. 500 rupees in 1994 was a lot of money. I unscrewed the top of the jar and, scooping out the alcohol with a serving spoon, poured it into a shot glass. "No way am I drinking that stuff!" Shareef said, backing away. "It stinks like sin." Suveer told him, "The Chinese minister who gave it to dad is ninety years old and sleeps with three women." So now we knew that the wine had a purpose. "Go, go, go..." we began to chant. Stepping forward, as if hypnotised by the snakes, Shareef chugged the shot. We all fell silent. We watched him gag and his face scrunch up, and his eyes open wide like they were about to pop out of his head.

He had the stench of death on his breath—the death of nine venomous snakes. We ran back to the comfort and security of our TV lounge and, blasting the music, danced wildly. Shareef lifted his arms above his head and made the hood of a cobra with his hands; he danced like a snake mesmerised by the flute of a Rajasthani snake charmer. What a night!

The snake wine, over the next few weeks, disappeared bit by bit, until only the snakes remained, sticking to each other in dear death. And then, one day, the jar was gone—the cook, Krishna, ecstatic that the liquor had finished, threw the lot of them out in a far corner of the garden. The snakes have become part of the farm now, part of the trees my children climb on, and the flowers the gardener plucks and arranges in the vases in our rooms. Luckily, they don't smell like the nine dead snakes, a smell etched into the membranes of my nose, never to be forgotten.

I suspect my brother and his girlfriend, a Thai girl by the name of Arinee, finished the lust-inducing alcoholic potion—or what the legend about the Chinese minister and his three concubines prevailed upon them was a lust-inducing potion. For I wouldn't see them out of his room, for days on end, until the last drop of the Nine Snake Wine was gone.

Day 61

20 May 2020

Potions, pills and occult fixes are all the rage in times of uncertainty. Quacks in Delhi are resorting to bizarre methods to make money off the fear-stricken populace; they're touting nasal drops to cure the killer virus, and charms and amulets to shield the wearer from it, as sure-shot remedies.

Illegal clinics are sprouting across the capital, offering quick fixes and bogus tests for the virus. To stop the menace, officials in the Delhi government have proposed to implement the Anti-Quackery Bill that was tabled years ago but not passed. An estimated 35,000 quacks have opened shop in the National Capital Region. They're putting people in harm's way by feeding on their fears. One person has died—a 45-year-old executive—because of the medication administered to him by a quack.

While Indians are making fools of Indians, a little old man in England is making rounds of his garden with his walker to raise funds to fight the virus in his country.

Captain Tom Moore, better known as Captain Tom, began making laps of his garden with the help of a walking frame, on 6 April, at the age of 99. His singular goal was to raise 1,000 pounds for the National Health Service by his 100th birthday. The media began covering him and the donations poured in. By the good captain's 100th birthday, the donations had crossed 30 million pounds. He received over 150,000 greeting cards and the Royal Air Force and the British Army conducted fly-pasts over his house to commemorate his big day. When he was knighted this week, he announced that he aims to do a second hundred rounds.

If only the quacks profiting from fear, and middlemen making a killing from the procurement of Personal Protective Equipment kits in Himachal Pradesh, Maharashtra and other places across India, were shamed and humbled by Captain Tom's selflessness and patriotism.

Day 62

21 May 2020

Never in the history of India has the country been more preoccupied with cleanliness than in the year 2020. People, who didn't wash their hands, as a norm, are washing them now, as if it was to save their lives—because it is.

The Minister of Civil Aviation has declared that domestic civil aviation operations will resume from 25 May. For this, extraordinary measures of cleanliness and hygiene are being deployed at Terminal 3 of the Indira Gandhi International Airport in New Delhi, from where all flights will take off. It is mandatory for all passengers to wear masks upon entering the aerodrome. After their temperatures are checked and they show their tickets and identification cards to the guard at the gate, standing behind a plexiglass shield, they will get to enter the building. They'll walk over a carpet coated with sanitiser to disinfect the soles of their shoes as they pass the double doors. Here, they will pause to undergo thermal screening. Queue managers inside the building will ensure that the passengers abide by the social distancing guidelines. Bags will be put into ultraviolet tunnels for disinfection. There will be markings around baggage belts, in lifts, on piers, aerobridges and chairs to ensure that the passengers stay 1 m apart. 500 sanitation professionals have been hired to sanitise counters, trolleys, chairs, baggage belts, elevators and railings on an hourly basis. Washrooms, too, will be cleaned every hour with UV and regular cleaners. Auto-dispensing sanitisers will be set up at counters, the terminal gate and in buses. 3,500 air-purifying indoor plants have been placed in the 608,000 sq m terminal. The air inside the building will be replaced every ten minutes. The Delhi International Airport Limited (DIAL) has said that, "A system has been put in place that sucks the air inside the terminal into the Air Handling Unit, where it gets sanitised after passing through UV light and HEPA filters, before being injected again into the terminal building." Security staff in masks and gloves will screen the airport staff. Cabin crew will wear Personal Protective Equipment kits on board the airplane. No measure has been overlooked in achieving cleanliness at the airport, but for a mandatory colon cleanse, or a strip search, like the one I was subjected to. (Jokes aside, I hope the measures implemented achieve the desired results.)

People have to understand the need for hygiene. They can't afford to treat the government's well-meaning initiatives like they did, for instance, the WAYU air purifiers installed on the city's intersections. The Delhi government, taking into consideration that Delhi is one of the highest polluters in the world, where 33 million people die each year from pollution, installed air purifiers around the city. The public soon turned these into dustbins and spittoons. They tossed cigarette butts, chewing gums, wires, and *bidis* and *gutka* packets into the purifying units.

We're not like the Japanese: cleanliness isn't in our DNA. Aside from droughts, famine, poor infrastructure, and the fact that we eat with our hands, not having the privilege of self-rule, for hundreds of years, could explain our modest levels of hygiene. We became used to being the invaded, the ruled, the vassals; we didn't have a sense of the land being ours, of our rights being ours, of a sense of responsibility for anything beyond the four walls of our homes or of our huts. But now, it's all ours. Nothing has brought that home like the pandemic of 2020 has. We have to be responsible for what is ours. We have to save ourselves. The best way, and frankly, the only way to do that right now, is to practice hygiene.

Day 63

22 May 2020

I heard Lakshmi squeak this evening. I can imagine how cooped up she must be feeling on her farm; it's not a big place, not for an elephant. She sees the same faces. She can't leave the property. She has no friends, not of her own kind, at least. I find myself identifying with her imaginable sense of seclusion; I feel like I was randomly selected from a fishnet full of souls and thrown into a group I don't belong in. The hand that swept me could have been tired: it performed this one anomalous act amidst the coordinated acts it is adept at performing. There is no love here: there are big cars, iron gates, brick walls, conflicting kitchens and a swimming pool. But for the pool, it's all beginning to suffocate me. I've been here 65 days. I miss my spouse. I miss my blind cat and miniature dog, and watering the plants on my balcony. I want to cry. I want to scream. I want to leave this habitat of garden and pond, flowers and fireflies, frogs and monkeys: having to contend with competitiveness and greed, spying servants, petty prattle, mountains made out of molehills, is clawing at my soul. With its juxtaposition of natural beauty and human frailty, this here, the farm, is a microcosm of the world.

I want to go back to that concrete jungle I used to call overcrowded and stinky; the claustrophobia I'm experiencing here has superseded that which I felt in that oceanside megalopolis. If only Mumbai didn't have so many daily cases! Hospitals and morgues are choking with bodies. The infected and the dead are becoming numbers of faceless nobodies. My building is in a hotspot; the street in front of it is cordoned off and its compound is sprayed daily by chemical disinfectants to protect its residents, including my husband who's on the 18th floor. He passes his time by singing to his fans on Facebook, writing poetry, feeding the birds and yelling at the cook who he's sick of dealing with (I ran the house before all this happened). Now *he's* having to supervise the cleaning and the cooking, and taking care of the pets. It gives me glee, I have to admit, to know the roles have reversed—at least for a while. He's lucky he doesn't have to rear the children along with managing the house! That housekeeping and childcare is a job in itself is an often-overlooked fact. I hope my husband's experience of it, limited as it is, makes him more appreciative of the role, and hence, of me; I hope he shares his insights with other married men who, like he was, are little acquainted with this aspect of their wives' experience. I always viewed that work as worth it, because, more than anything, it is my family unit that makes me tick.

The pandemic has torn my heart between the two cities. To mend it, I can do nothing but wait. I'm sure my time to return to that city by the ocean will come; sure as the salt in its coastal waters.

Day 64

23 May 2020

New Delhi's stringent lockdown has been lifted for the first time in 65 days. I ventured beyond a 4 km radius. Listening to Nirvana, I drove to Central Market.

Hello, hello, hello, how low
Hello, hello, hello

With the lights out, it's less dangerous
Here we are now, entertain us
I feel stupid and contagious
Here we are now, entertain us
A mulatto, an albino, a mosquito, my libido...

As my car turned onto the main avenue of the market, I saw the "nowhere people". It wasn't like seeing them on the news, where they were first termed the "nowhere people", or like on social media or donation drives: it was real. The "nowhere people" are the people the pandemic has chewed up and spat out; the daily wagers, migrant workers, the cannon fodder in this war against what the foreign news anchors call "the invisible enemy". Standing in the kilometre-long queue were mostly men, mostly young men, wearing blue caps sitting awkwardly on their heads, presumably donated by some NGO. Policemen were coaxing them with their *lathis* to keep them in a straight line. The heat is at a constant 45 degree Celsius. Stepping outside is like stepping into an oven; the sun bakes the skin to a barbecue red. The men were getting baked halfway to their bones.

I miss you, I'm not gonna crack
I love you, I'm not gonna crack
I killed you, I'm not gonna crack

I'm so happy 'cause today I found my friends
They're in my head
I'm so ugly, but that's okay, 'cause so are you
Broke our mirrors
Sunday morning is everyday, for all I care...

The "nowhere people" carried that godawful look that the lost and surrendered carry. I wanted to give them a lift to wherever they wished to go. I wanted to tell them that everything would be alright. The wheels of my car kept rolling; for I could do nothing but watch.

No salesman, shop owner, pedestrian or passerby in the market had a happy face. Everyone was going through the motions to get through the day.

I drove to different markets to buy the things I needed; to Central Market for cloth and elastic to make masks, to Evergreen in Defence Colony for medicines, and to MG Road, not far from home, to buy groceries. I parked my car beside the liquor store in the village near my house: I wanted chilled beer to cool me down and to make me numb to what I had seen in the day. As I stepped out of the vehicle, I noticed, to my satisfaction, that there were no customers at the store, but just as I reached the counter, I was suddenly swamped by 20 men. The salespeople were as surprised as I was by the influx. The policemen standing nearby—there are policemen, even now, at every corner—raised their *lathis* to get everyone in line. The men had seen a tall brunette with light eyes approaching the disreputable store. What they didn't see, however, because of the mask covering half of her face, was her age. She was 46 years old.

I've been thinking a lot about masks and identity. A woman in a burqa leaves to the imagination of a man what wonders lie beneath her veil. We're all going to be like those men, who try to visualise the woman hidden in the fabric. Since our faces will be half-covered for most of the year, we will have to peer into the windows of the soul, the eyes, to take a guess at the character behind the mask. Blocked from seeing facial expressions that are capable of deceiving, mocking or misleading, there will be less to go by; but less will be more: the eyes will reveal the truth—even in the words.

Day 65

24 May 2020

I enjoyed the pleasure of having dinner and wine with a friend for the first time in over two months. Blowing kisses to each when we met, rather than embracing, as we usually do, felt a bit weird; but all else was like any other visit to her house. Her five dogs, half Chihuahua and half Pekingese, snuggled up to me on the couch, glancing up at me with their angelic eyes when I talked too much and forgot to pet them.

Jia is ten years older than me. I consider her the sister I never had. She's sensitive, sophisticated and smart. And, boy, does she know how to eat healthy! We had carrot soup, quinoa salad and baked fish for dinner, and for dessert, we had home-made mango sorbet.

This evening of normal life fitted oddly into the larger context; even the smallest experiences, these past few months have reminded me, come within a framework. Being in the company of positive people, in a comfortable bubble, won't guarantee you an escape from the energy of the billions of people living in fear or grief. The toxicity that the pandemic has spread is like the black smoke that factories using rubber as fuel emit. Empowering gravity, the negativity pulls you down, as if you're carrying an extra five kilos. In the first days of the disease in India, a politician and his party workers held a vigil, shaking their fists in the air, chanting through the night, "Go.... Go.... Go...," as if the virus would go away by their willing it to go, or commanding it to go. I'm an outraged avatar of that lot: I'm chanting, "Be gone, you damn pestilence!"

I find myself making promises that I have every intention of keeping, but I'm not sure that I, nor the rest of my species, are capable of keeping; such as, "I will stop polluting the planet. I will stop eating wild or mass-produced meat. I won't travel unless I have to. I'll carpool. I'll limit my use of plastics. I'll be empathetic; I'll care about my planet; I'll be considerate of the creatures that live on it, because they have the same rights to it that I do." I'm making these promises because I miss my friends. I miss my family. I miss a tender touch. And now, I'm going to go back to the top of this passage and count how many "I's" there are in it.

Day 69

28 May 2020

"Strength is Life, Weakness is Death," said Swami Vivekananda. We've been so busy dealing with the pandemic that we've not been able to pay attention to other evils we commonly work to suppress. The wicked and the ignorant are taking advantage of this; they're growing in confidence. Between 42 and 66 million more children are likely to be added to the 152 million children already in the workforce. The most vulnerable are the children of minoritics, migrants, refugees, and children with disabilities; and that's because they are generally malnourished and lack access to adequate water to practice hygiene or space to exercise social distancing. To boost the family income, they will have to quit school and work in the fields (most child labour is in agriculture).

In Africa, where the virus is spreading fast, a steep rise has been observed in Female Genital Mutilation (FGM). Cutters are going from house to house to be utilised in the barbaric practice. With no government regulation and NGOs having difficulty in reaching the villages and raising funds, the practice is flourishing, especially in Somalia.

China has transgressed along the Line of Actual Control (LAC) in four places in Ladakh. A heavy build-up of Chinese troops and trucks in these locations has put the Indian Army on alert. Analysts say that the Chinese are trying to send a message domestically as well as externally. This makes sense, considering how they've appropriated islands in the South and East China Sea and are posturing in Taiwan. The riot police were deployed in Hong Kong as hundreds of pro-democracy protesters, aged 12 to 65, spilled onto the streets to demonstrate against the new bill proposed by Xi Jinping and approved by the Chinese parliament.

The National Security Law (NSL) promises "tougher measures on those deemed as harbouring secessionist views, and codifies China's right to use national troops and national security agencies in Hong Kong," writes author and journalist, Adam Withnall, in the *Independent*. Calling the imposition of this Law "the beginning of the end of Hong Kong", he opined that it would effectively invalidate the notion of "one country, two systems".

The recent transgressions by China are part of its policy of using aggression to achieve world domination. In response to a senior general in the Chinese Army declaring that China would claim Taiwan by force if the island became independent, the Taiwanese government said, "Taiwan has never been a part of the People's Republic of China," and "Taiwan's people will never choose dictatorship nor bow to violence." This is not like David taking on Goliath: this is like an ant taking on a gorilla.

China has a landmass of 9.597 million sq km, whereas Taiwan has a landmass of 36,193 sq km. China has a population of 1.428 billion people, whereas Taiwan's population is 2.38 crore. The island country is an inspiration! We, as a sisterhood of nations, shouldn't forget how China behaved during this worst time for our global family. It has not behaved like the spoilt child who throws a tantrum to get his way but the stepfather who uses the belt to enforce his authority. We can't have that—not in this family. China needs to simmer down, or else—come on, there *has to be* an or else!

Day 70

29 May 2020

The 400-year-old disease of racism at the core of America, ever on the verge of turning cancerous and incapacitating the system, has, once again, reared its head. A police officer killed an African–American man by pressing him against the ground with his knee upon his neck. The man pleaded for his life, called out for his mother, and asked the policeman to let him stand up, but the cop continued applying pressure on his neck until, nine minutes later, the man was dead. The modern-day lynching took place in broad daylight and in the presence of three other officers. The only aspect that differentiated it from the lynching in the old days, in the deep South, was the costume of the perpetrator; the white cape of the Ku Klux Klan (KKK) had been replaced by the blue uniform of the white police.

When the officer who killed George Floyd in Minneapolis was not arrested for four days, peaceful demonstrations turned angry. The outrage manifested in a fire at a gas station and a police station. The demonstrations spread to New York, New Orleans, Atlanta, Dallas, Houston, Portland, Los Angeles, Oakland, Boston, Denver, Washington, D.C. and Detroit. The protesters caused extensive property damage. The fired officer was charged with third-degree murder and manslaughter, and the three officers who looked on and did nothing, will be charged, too, in the coming days. This was good news. But because the momentum of the protests was high by the time the decision came, demonstrations continued.

When Trump held a press conference, at long last, instead of speaking about the unlawful killing in police custody of an African-American man and the subsequent nation-wide unrest, he spoke about China's crackdown on secessionist demonstrators in Hong Kong and the passing of the new legislation restricting its autonomy. No mention of the name George Floyd. I'd call the content of his speech random, if only it was; Trump had intentionally designed his speech to make no mention of the murder of a black man by a white policeman. He also refused to take questions from the media.

The US is going to the polls in November. Donald Trump has to please his vote base, the majority of which are white Americans. This is Trump's America. He wants it to continue to be Trump's America. He can do as he pleases, say what he pleases, grab whoever he pleases by whatever body parts he pleases, because he has millions who support him. One of those millions was an individual who shot into the crowd of black demonstrators from a car and killed a 19-year-old man in Detroit. White America. Supremacist America. Trump's America. No beating into sameness here by the virus: more blacks are dying from it, and also from the endemic racism it has allowed to grow.

George Floyd's last words were, "I can't breathe." The earth has been crying out, "I can't breathe," for a while now. Patients suffering from the virus complain, "I can't breathe." These three words have become the slogan of the era. When we *all* can't breathe behind the masks that we're being forced to wear, I hope to God that we will, finally, have enough empathy to hear the cries of the earth and its creatures, the minorities, the displaced and the impoverished, and stop being so selfish.

Day 71

30 May 2020

While one of the three astronauts in space has returned to earth, two others took flight from NASA's Kennedy Space Station, in what's called the Dragon Spacecraft. The craft, which was manufactured by Elon Musk's company, SpaceX, has the safest and most advanced systems on board. This was the first time in nine years that humans took flight into space from US soil, and, that too, on a commercial shuttle. Flying at 17,000 miles per hour, the spacecraft will take 19 hours to deliver the astronauts to the International Space Station. It's likely that the spacewalkers will stay there for upwards of 120 days. The success of this mission will mean a lot of things for a lot of people.

For one, it will prove actor Tom Cruise's dream to shoot a movie on the space station achievable. It will also get travellers a step closer to vacationing in orbit. While Shramik trains crisscross the Indian subcontinent, deployed for the special purpose of transporting the unfortunate victims of the pandemic back to their home states, the astronauts will look upon a tranquil view of the earth, the same view as always, ravaged by disease or not. The sky's the limit for the virus but not for humankind's dreams. This mission will lay the grounds for future missions to the moon, Mars, and beyond.

I've begun to believe that relocating humans to other planets is necessary. We've been wrecking our planet for a while, and it seems unlikely that we'll stop, even after this disease is done with its destruction. Pandemics, climate change, cyber warfare: too many maladies that need grappling with and too little incentive to do the grappling. It's easier to resign to fate. We're lazy. We're greedy. We're habitual. We're too lazy to stop being greedy—we're habituated to it. Visionaries like Elon Musk realise that getting China to change its policies is a formidable task that no singular leader, genius or demigod, can achieve. It will take the coming together of *all* the world leaders to restrain the red dragon. And it's not only China, but other nations, too, that are cause for worry.

We're seeing dictators rising to power, everywhere, playing partisan politics and wreaking havoc on the social and environmental climate. It could be that people like me are naive to think that things can change for the better after this scourge, that we will learn, that we will reform. The visionaries know better. Duh! That's why they're called visionaries. I fall into the "hopefuls" category—the hopefuls who scream from rooftops and roadsides, vehemently protesting the status quo and managing to get little done, despite all their efforts. Colonising space may be the only way to go for humanity. It may be the only way to preserve civilisation. The question is—is it worth preserving?

Day 73

1 June 2020

Written in large letters with red mineral, on the side of a mud hut, is the Hindi word for hunger, *bhookh*. It was made by a starving man in Bundelkhand, one of the poorest regions in the country, which happens to be in a state governed by a yogi. One would naturally assume that someone as apparently pious as the Chief Minister in orange robes would be affected by the suffering of the poor in his state; not so in this case though—the yogi's primary goals are to build a temple and stop cow slaughter (regardless of how those cows are surviving in shelters on inadequate food and veterinary care). It is said that the main purpose of a yogi is to go beyond the physical aspect; this yogi, however, is preoccupied with building a megalithic statue and a house of God: nothing gets more physical than a structure capable of standing for aeons.

The cost of the temple and the statue will be borne by the poor: they will pay for it with their lives—lives that extinguish invisibly, like puffs of air in a mist. According to the Hindu school of philosophy, Advaita Vedanta, God resides within every living being as *atman* or soul. Each one of us, thus, is the house of God. The job of a leader of the people is to preserve the people, first and foremost. To ignore the needs of the poor, by a leader responsible for their well-being—especially if that leader is a yogi—is to ignore God. The starving Bundelkhandi man died after writing the word on the wall. Shoving a microphone in his face, a journalist asked the man's five-year-old son, "Who wrote this?" The boy replies, "Papa." He places a tender hand on his three-year-old brother's shoulder. The journalist probes further, "Why did he write it?" Turning away in shame—shame he had no reason to feel, not him, but his Chief Minister—the boy says, "Because we don't have food."

Straggly children in dusty underwear lie in a bunch amid a circle made by their parents demonstrating in the village courtyard; their limbs flopped on the ground, they lack the energy children their age normally have. Everyone here is hungry. The famine predicted by the experts has begun. This is its first destination, and the man who wrote the word for hunger on the side of his hut, its first claim. The problem, on a microcosmic level, is that the government declared that people who don't have ration cards, and therefore access to food, should be given provisional cards and supplied with food grains, but this is harder to do than to declare because of the rampant corruption at the village level; the cards can't be procured without giving a bribe. Complaints were filed about this by the villagers at the District Magistrate's office and even at the Chief Minister's portal. There was no response; the apathy continues.

The forgotten people remain forgotten. The influx of migrant workers returning to their villages is causing social tension, as the supply of food is scarce in the region. NGOs operating in rural areas are warning of a humanitarian crisis. The crisis has started; farmers are committing suicide and abandoning their cows. The cause of Bundelkhand's backwardness is poor irrigation systems, and long periods of drought compounded by erratic weather. The reason why these causes are not addressed—and this is the problem on a macrocosmic level—is because of caste politics, systemic corruption and bureaucratic indifference.

What I fail to understand is, why the word *bhookh* on a mud-hut wall and the man who wrote it dying of hunger in plain sight of his children, who are likely to follow him, isn't angering us into a frenzy. Why aren't we demonstrating against this death, the first of many to come, like we did at the time of the Nirbhaya rape? Are we so scared of the virus that we'd rather watch men, women and children of our country die of hunger than come out on the streets and demand accountability and action from the government?

The statue of a god, that the yogi with the 600 dollar Ray-Bans intends to build alongside the temple in Ayodhya, will be the tallest in the world, taller than the one Narendra Modi built of Sardar Vallabhbhai Patel in Gujarat. Modi's statue is twice the height of the Statue of Liberty; I'm guessing it's his way of telling Trump, "Donaaaald, mine is bigger than yours." Men with big egos make big things, and mostly at the expense of the little people. The land Modi's statue stands on, overarching the river and the forests and estuaries, big enough to eat them all, was snatched from the Adivasi and indigenous people, for whom the land was sacred. The Gujarat government spent 2,989 crore to build the statue of India's first Deputy Prime Minister.

The yogi's message to the PM appears to be, "Narendra, mine is not only bigger than yours but also firmer than yours." His statue will stand 16 m taller than the Prime Minister's and will be made in bronze. Mayawati, the former Chief Minister of Uttar Pradesh, a woman not exempt from having an ego as big as the men, spent 2,600 crore on erecting statues of herself and elephants, parks and memorials. The statues she sanctioned of herself are exact replicas, having a boxy face and a boxy body with a boxy haircut and holding a boxy bag. All this money going into building statues when people are dying of hunger!

Mr Prime Minister, where is your 20 lakh crore relief package going? Where are the collections from the Prime Minister's Fund going? The money can't only be going into the Shramik trains returning the migrant workers to their home states. What's happening with the testing, tracing and surveillance strategy for curbing the spread of the virus? The Fund was meant for combatting the epidemic. There isn't enough testing happening. Patients in government quarantine facilities don't have food and water; they are running away from the facilities. How many statues are we going to erect at the expense of the poor? Shouldn't we ensure that everyone has food, water, and clean toilets for their sanitary needs, before erecting monuments of dead people or intangible entities?

What happened to saving the living? Prime Minister, why so quiet? Come out from behind the pristine walls of 7 Lok Kalyan Marg and answer the pertinent questions. Announcing a lockdown and delegating funds isn't enough: you are accountable for where the funds go; every last rupee is precious. If you don't make sure the money is going to those who need it the most, the fate of the Bundelkhand man who wrote *bhookh* on the wall of his mud hut before dying from hunger, and of his sons, his wife, his neighbours, and the folk in the next village, will be due to your negligence. Can you, sir, live with this on your conscience?

Day 75

3 June 2020

Locals, living at the edge of a forest in Kerala, packed a pineapple with firecrackers and fed it to a pregnant elephant standing in the river. The pineapple exploded in her mouth. By the time forest officials arrived at the site, she was head under, dying a slow and agonising death. 11,000 elephants have died in the past six years in the state we call "God's Own Country". Every third day, an elephant is killed in India. The locals see the wildlife that encroaches on their land—land they took from the forest—as vermin. In the same week this incident happened, in Silent Valley, the only evergreen forest left in South India, the Chief Minister of the state proposed the construction of a 120 ft tall statue of Swami Vivekananda. As much as I revere the spiritual leader, I don't see how a statue of him will save the endangered animals and the dying forests and rivers of the state.

I'm sure that an aesthetically pleasing 100 ft statue can garner the same admiration as a 220 m statue. We don't need to look upon a colossus to be reminded of the contribution the inspirational men and women they're fashioned on, made to mankind—we can do that on Google. What we really should be doing is reading the teachings of these individuals and about how they lived their lives, and aspire to be like them. I'm sure all these great people, with the exception of Mayawati, would have preferred the thousands of crores spent on making their statues had gone into empowering the poor of the nation and preserving its forests and animals.

Day 77

5 June 2020

"Mom, what are you looking at?" Rishi called out from the shallow end of the pool. I was in the cool waters of the deep, my chin resting on the side, watching a high-speed chase. Limbs outstretched, body parallel to the ground, a monkey leapt from the wall to a branch. He flew seven feet. Bingo! It was this capability of a rhesus macaque that inspired the earliest imaginations of a proto-Hanuman, as described in the Rig Veda; I was sure of it. I recalled the illustrations from the Amar Chitra Katha comics of my childhood, of Hanuman flying across the ocean to Lanka.

In some texts, including the Ramayana, Hanuman never died and never left the earth. It's not hard to believe, for me. I see him every day, in Patlu and Jaggu, the alpha males who battle over territory around the pool. Hanuman is the god of strength, celibacy and intellect. Monkeys are one of the most sexually playful creatures. That Hanuman is celibate despite being a primate points to his tremendous self-control. Mastery over the mind distinguishes an evolved being from one who exists on a baser level; this mastery, or self-control, makes one Godlike. When I see Patlu slip into the pool and surface on the other side, without gasping for breath, I think of a little-known story from the Ramayana, about Hanuman.

The mermaid, Suvannamaccha, was the daughter of the demon king, Ravana. She, and her mermaid friends, used to steal the rocks that Rama's Army of monkeys tossed into the sea to build a bridge to Lanka. Hanuman dove into the water and swam to Suvannamaccha to persuade her to stop stealing the rocks and let them build the bridge. He remained underwater with her for several days. When I hear Patlu and Jaggu roar at each other, I can understand why Hanuman's roar is so famous.

An excerpt from the Hindu-Pagan Society's interpretation of the Hanuman Chalisa reads, "When you roar, all the three worlds tremble, and only you can control your might." Hanuman's roar is the reason why Arjuna had a flag with Hanuman's image attached to his chariot when he entered war. Hanuman's image on the flag, it is said, intensified Arjuna's war cry. I've seen Jaggu and Patlu get into vociferous battles; grunting, hollering and hooting. When the two actually get down to fighting, they inflict grievous injuries upon each other.

Watching these miniature versions of the Monkey God flying, swimming and fighting, I sometimes feel like I'm in His presence. My son called out, "Mom, didn't you hear me? What are you looking at?" Swimming back to him, I said, "Son, I think I saw Hanuman, flying from the wall to a tree."

"Hanuman!" he said. "You mean, the God?"

"Yes," I replied, "the God in all monkeys, like Patlu and Jaggu, and in little boys like you."

Day 78

6 June 2020

"My mommy is quarantined at home. My daddy is dead. I feel helpless," says the girl on television. WTF! Where have we got ourselves! Why can't we do the right thing? "Turn to faith," the evangelists say on television. I wrote this poem out of frustration at our species:

The old are dying,
The young are dying,
No dignity,
No respect for life,
Vacant, empty beds,
Beds with corpses,
Or no beds.
This, while we all pray,
"As long as it's not me."

Day 79

7 June 2020

I called the manager of Lakshmi's farm to inquire about her. She has been locked within the walls of her 5 acre farm for close to three months. My only connection with her is the squeaks I hear in the evening, when it's her mealtime. Despite her seclusion, she's still the lucky one—hundreds of captive elephants are starving and many have died across India during the pandemic. All elephants are facing an uncertain future.

I've had an affinity with elephants since childhood. I have a tattoo of Ganesha on my back. The most extraordinary story I know about the animal comes from South Africa. There was a herd of elephants that had been rampaging through electrical fences and into crop fields. The farmers in the region came to consider them "rogue" wild elephants. When they learned that the pachyderms had strayed out of the protected areas, hunters gathered from all over South Africa to kill them. Half the herd had already been killed, or culled, as it's normally called—the allowance of an elephant to be killed by hunters if it strays out of its protected area. The herd was traumatised. Their matriarch had been killed and the new matriarch was confused about where to lead the herd. She was trying to find safe lands for them. Conservation activists turned to South African author and conservationist, Lawrence Anthony. They asked him to take the herd into his Thula Thula Game Reserve in Zululand. Lawrence knew that if he didn't take the elephants in, they would be killed by the big game hunters.

The herd was aggressive. They got agitated whenever humans came near them. Every night, the matriarch, Nana, tried to lead the herd off the property by ploughing through the electric fence. Over a period of three weeks, Lawrence camped closer and closer to the fence. Early every morning, he would stand by the fence and block Nana's way, whispering to her, warning her about the dangers that lay beyond the fences. Then, one day, Nana reached over the fence with her trunk and touched Lawrence's head. After this physical interaction, she stopped trying to lead the herd off Thula Thula, and decided to make it home.

Thirteen years after Nana accepted Lawrence into the family fold, he died of a heart attack in his house on the edge of the reserve. The herd was thousands of acres away at the time. They walked for 12 hours through Zululand bush and reached his house in the KwaZulu province. For two days, they held a vigil outside his house and mourned the loss of their friend. It has been eight years now since Lawrence died. The herd continues to visit his house each year on the anniversary of his death. Thanks to the efforts of this remarkable man, who came to be known as the Elephant Whisperer, the herd is three times the size.

This story clearly indicates that elephants have telepathic capabilities; and that they have sympathy, loyalty and trust—trust, even after experiencing betrayal and grief. Nana and her herd accepted Lawrence despite their traumatic experiences with humans. This attests their capacity for forgiveness. The story begs the question: if wild animals can accept human beings, why on earth can't we humans live alongside wild animals instead of grabbing their land?

Day 90

18 June 2020

Despite the vacillations in my views on human nature in the past few months, since the virus arrived in India, I believe that the pandemic has strengthened our collective ability to empathise and assert ourselves. It has kicked us into consciousness; it's given our insensitivity to everything but our own desires a jolt. That the demonstrations against George Floyd's lynching went global is case in point; aside from demonstrations, statues of figures of colonialism and slave traders, internationally, were smeared with red paint, or desecrated.

"A riot is the language of the unheard," said Martin Luther King. Demonstrations against injustice and apathy are happening everywhere. Venetians made a human chain in Venice demanding "responsible tourism". Hong Kong's pro-democracy protests continue despite the pandemic. America and India have imposed sanctions against China in response to its transgressions into Indian territory. While in lockdown, inventors focused on creating sustainable alternatives to products and systems that pollute and degrade the environment. The suspicion that the virus is related to the climate crisis, and the related loss in biodiversity, has given the need to remedy the problem of climate change far more urgency.

"We need big thinking and big changes," says Professor Phoebe Koundouri, in her opinion piece (1 April 2020), 'Never Waste a Good Crisis: For a Sustainable Recovery from Covid-19'. Because using science to combat the virus is the only way to control its spread and the number of deaths caused by it, and indeed, to put an end to it, more of us have realised that scientific data just can't be ignored. Koundouri, Founder and Scientific Director of the Research Laboratory on Socio-Economic and Environmental Sustainability (ReSEES), writes, "We can use science to design economies that will mitigate the threats of climate change, biodiversity loss, and pandemics."

She proposes that we "start investing in what makes our socio-economic system resilient to crisis, by laying the foundation for a green, circular economy that is anchored in nature-based solutions and geared toward public well-being". She says that "such policies, if implemented efficiently, could be imperceptive in the daily lives of most people and businesses". That's the good news, that last bit, because it means that all we, the people, have to do to kick-start the necessary changes, is to vote in the right leaders. By voting in capable and good people to lead the way, we can leverage our power to achieve, what Koundouri describes as "the vision of a prosperous, inclusive, climate and pandemic resilient society with a circular net-zero emissions economy".

Many of us are developing a taste for a life of simplicity, regardless that we were forced into it and thereby became habituated to it. Many of us don't want to go back to the status quo after the pandemic subsides. The health crisis has shown us that all we really need are the essentials. The innovators are waiting—they're waiting for us to elect the right leaders to give them the signal to begin the transformation. What *we* can do, till then, each one of us, on a personal level, is to continue with what we've been doing these past few months—keep to the essentials. If we can condition ourselves to stick to the essentials, we will thrive as a species, and so will our precious earth.

References

hindustantimes.com/india/rajiv-gandhi-s-sri-lanka-policy-led-to-his-death-natwar-singh/story-0JLTRSHTUF92n32q904rnl.html

firstpost.com/india/chandraswami-the-life-and-times-of-self-styled-godman-who-became-controversys-favourite-child-3475296.html

m-english.webdunia.com/article/hinduism-spiritual-leaders/did-chandraswami-fund-the-killing-of-rajiv-gandhi-116081300012_1.html?amp=1

history.co.uk/shows/ancient-aliens/articles/do-aliens-exist-most-compelling-evidence-of-alien-existence

timesofindia.indiatimes.com/travel/things-to-do/delhi-airport-takes-impressive-measures-to-provide-safe-environment-for-passengers-after-lockdown-is-over/as75364930.cms

aninews.in/news/national/general-news/delhi-airport-authorities-make-special-arrangements-to-resume-operations-from-march-2520200523155948/

magzter.com/stories/Newspaper/Mail-Today/Quacks-Make-A-Killing-With-Covid-Cures

en.m.wikipedia.org/wiki/Captain_Tom_Moore

diffuser.fm/best-nirvana-lyrics/

theprint.in/defence/Chinese-in-Ladakh-also-a-messge-for-domestic-and-external-audience-experts/431286/

independent.co.uk/author/adam-withnall

independent.co.uk/independentpremium/world/china-national-security-law-hong-kong-congress-a9528506.html

economictimes.indiatimes.com/news/defence/attack-on-taiwan-an-option-to-stop-independence-top-China-general-says/articleshow/76088758.cms

washingtonpost.com/nation/2020/05/30/george-floyd-protests-live-updates/

hindustantimes.com/india-news/over-1-4-stranded-migrant-workers-repatriated-1074-shramik-special-trains-operated-till-may-15-midnight-indian-railways/story-8mkTQIYqohxkfK2dexVT3J.html

nationalheraldindia.com/india/hunger-again-stalks-bundelkhand-as-reverse-migration-puts-pressure-on-food-supply

theconversation.com/india-unveils-the-worlds-tallest-statue-celebrating-development-at-the-cost-of-the-environment-105731#:~:text=India's%20Prime%20Minister%20Narendra%20Modi,Prime%20Minister%2C%20Sardar%20Vallabhbhai%20Patel

economictimes.indiatimes.com/news/politics-and-nation/mayawati-has-to-pay-for-statues-supreme-court/articleshow/67897118.cms?from=mdr

ndtv.com/india-news/yogi-adityanaths-planned-lord-ram-statue-at-251-metres-worlds-tallest-2073854

google.com/search?q=What+is+the+estimated+cost+of+Yogi+Adityanath%27s+Ram+statue+in+Ayodhya%3F&rlz=1C5CHFA_enIN902IN902&oq=What+is+the+estimated+cost+of+Yogi+Adityanath%27s+Ram+statue+in+Ayodhya%3F&aqs=chrome..69i57.34488j0j4&sourceid=chrome&ie=UTF-8

en.wikipedia.org/wiki/Hanuman#:~:text=The%20earliest%20mention%20of%20a,between%201500%20and%201200%20BCE

ancient.eu/Hanuman/

en.wikipedia.org/wiki/Suvannamaccha

spacex.com/launches/

youtube.com/watch?v=Tjp_nPRtCLo

en.wikipedia.org/wiki/Golden_Rule

thefederal.com/news/behind-ppe-supply-irregularities-anomalies-and-alleged-scams/

unsdsn.org/never-waste-a-good-crisis-for-a-sustainable-recovery-from-covid-19

A.C. Bhaktivedanta Swami Prabhupāda, *Coming Back: The Science of Reincarnation*, Mumbai, The Bhaktivedanta Book Trust, 1984

Acknowledgements

I want to thank my English teacher, Ms Kathy Hoffmann, for always reminding me in class that if I wasn't such a noisemaker I could be a good writer. Additionally, my thanks to Mr Ranjit Dass, my history teacher and high-school coordinator, for expressing faith in me and encouraging me in all my endeavours during my formative years.

I owe a debt of gratitude to my literary agent, Suhail Mathur, of The Book Bakers and the team at Om Books International for enabling this book to reach the discerning reader.

I thank my friends who gave me moral, professional and emotional support in the course of writing this book: Janhavi Prasada, Annie Anand, Jayashree Chadha, Natascha Chadha, Deepa Vishwanathan, Vikram Kashyap, Shweta Sethi (Tina), Courtney Le Vasseur, Chris Miller, Alia Gulati and Samantha Kochharr.